The Keystone Legacy: Reflections of a Black Pioneer

Gwen Hooks

Brightest Pebble
Publishing Co. Inc.
1997

To My Loving Family

First Printing, June 1997 by:
Art Design Printing Inc., Edmonton Alberta, Canada

Cover design by Art Design

First published in 1997 by
Brightest Pebble Publishing Co. Ltd.
7604 - 149 Avenue
Edmonton, Alberta, Canada
T5C 2V7
Telephone (403) 457-7496
Fax (403) 475-0243

Canadian Cataloguing in Publication Data

Hooks,Gwen 1920

The Keystone Legacy: Recollections of a Black Settler

Includes bibliographical references and index

ISBN 0-9699669-4-6

1. Black Canadians—Canada, Western—History. 2. Black Canadians—Alberta—Breton—History. 3. Blacks—Canada, Western—History 4. Blacks—Alberta—Breton—History 5. Canada, Western—History. 6. Breton (Alta.)—History. I. Title

FC3699.B74Z7 1997   971.2'00496   C97-900558-2
F1079.5B74H66 1997

This book is based mainly on the memories of people who witnessed first hand the events told in this book or who knew people who did. I recognize the problem of accuracy in memory reaching back a half-century and more. Therefore, I cannot guarantee that everything written in this book is accurate. I took some liberties and made some assumptions based on information that was not always complete.

Contents

About the Author

Gwen Hooks is a graduate of the University of Alberta and a retired public school teacher who spends much of her time researching and writing, especially about Black heritage and pioneer times.

She presently makes her home in Leduc, Alberta, after having lived most of her life on a farm near Breton, Alberta.

Aside from her family, her first love is poetry. After retiring from teaching, she attended poetry conventions in Washington D.C., New York, and Las Vegas and has won awards for her poetry.

Gwen and her late husband, Mark, have always lived active lives and have been involved in organizations such as the Farmers' Union of Alberta, the Warburg Royal Canadian Legion and Auxiliary, the Warburg Elks, the Breton Chamber of Commerce, and the Breton and District Historical Society of which Gwen served as president for many years.

Acknowledgements

I would like particularly to acknowledge the encouragement I have received from four persons in the writing of this book. My sons, Wayne and Terry and their wives both named Gail as well as my grandchildren Karen, Adam, Tyler, and Devon. My publisher Jim Musson and his colleagues Phyllis Schmitt and Lynn Oberle have provided me with the expertise that helped me research, write, and edit this book that could not have been completed without them. Hattie (Robinson) Collins, Harvey Bailey, the Ross girls, Addie Proctor, Vant and Mellie Hays, Mildred Gerrard, Willard and Marguerite Robinson, and Nellie Whalen who is presently working on a book that will highlight black heritage in Alberta. I am also grateful to Lloyd Ellis for possessing the forsight to take and collect pictures of Breton's heritage, many of which are now in the Breton Museum.

Thanks to past and present board members of the Breton & District Historical Society whose efforts to keep the Keystone and Breton heritage alive is very much appreciated. The present members include Alma and Don Gillies, Allan Goddard, Lee Hansen, Effie Nanninga, Margaret Rustand, and Linda and Tom Wall. Thanks also to Charlene Wheale of Wheale Photographics for reproducing several of the pictures used in this book. Others too numerous to mention have given me support and the full benefit of their knowledge of Keystone's legacy to make this book possible.

But a very special thanks goes to my late husband Mark. Without him this book would naver have been written. He was the inspiration. He loved his Breton home and cherished the legacy handed down to him from his pioneer parents. He always wanted to write a book about that legacy but death intervened before he could fullfill that dream. In my own humble way I have tried to fullfill it for him, but I came to the task as an amateur and I realize there are errors and omissions for which I ask the reader to be generous and forgiving.

**The Production of this book
was funded in part by the
Alberta Historical
Resources Foundation**

Chapter 1
Pre-Oklahoma

Clicks of wheels on steel beat a monotonous cadence to the rhythmic sway of rail cars. Day and night the clicks seldom ceased except when the train stopped to take on water and coal. A shriek, like finger nails over a blackboard, and a hiss of steam told the weary travellers that they could leave their cars, stretch their legs and get a breath of fresh air. Then the journey would resume.

Merged with the clicks came the sound of children playing in the aisle, laughing and bawling. Some cooed quietly in their mothers' arms. Women chatted and complained of their hardships and speculated on what their lives would be like in Canada. There was optimism, but it was guarded. There had been so many disappointments before. Would Canada really be the promised land? Time would tell.

On the train blacks suffered no segregation because it was a special train carrying only blacks. It pulled eight to ten cars including three coaches. Women and children rode in the cramped coaches, while the men rode in special box cars with the machinery and livestock they were bringing to Canada. Like a miniature Noah's Ark, there were horses, mules, cows, chickens, and numerous other animals as well as valuable possessions—heirlooms and special pieces of furniture that simply couldn't be left behind. There was farm equipment of every description. William (Buddy) Robinson, my wife Gwen's uncle, even brought his cotton gin. If nothing else, it would serve as a great conversation piece and a reminder of another place, another home, another dream gone sour. During the early days of the Keystone settlement, he built a table around it.

My mother, Neoma, father Sam Hooks, sisters Virginia (Virgie), and Victoria, and two brothers Ellis, and Elmer, and my maternal grandmother came to Canada from Sharpes, Oklahoma, in 1911 to seek freedom and a better life. The rest of our family stayed in Oklahoma.

In Sharpes County, cotton, wheat, peanuts, and sorghum for fodder were the main crops. Many blacks toiled sunup to sundown pulling heavy bags of cotton behind them—a backbreaking job. I can remember my wife's father Willis Day from Okmulgee saying, "I never want to see another field of cotton." He had worked in the cotton field from the time he was five years old until he and his family left Oklahoma to come to Alberta. In later years when he took a trip to Arizona, he refused to visit a cotton field in bloom. He, like most other black immigrants, was tired of slaving on land owned by others. There was no future for them in Oklahoma, and they wanted their own land.

Dad was about five foot seven, well built, and very strong. He always smoked a pipe. I can remember the strong sweet smell of tobacco when he was home. He was in his early twenties when he arrived in Canada. Neither he nor mother had ever lived in slavery, but they suffered their share of discrimination.

Neoma, my mother, was born in Muskogee, Oklahoma, in 1887. This was also cotton country. She was the fifth child of a family of eight, and she was around eighteen when she and Dad were married. Being part Creek, she spoke Cree fluently. When natives came by the homestead, she often conversed with them in their own language. She loved to sing and she sang hymns all the time. She was a very religious, quiet, and unexcitable woman who loved her children. When faced with an emergency, she always knew what to do. After an emergency or serious illness, she would always say, "It's best you don't remember."

We were not the first blacks to come to Alberta, but we were among a very small minority who came in a wave of immigration between 1908-1914, mostly from Oklahoma. We left our homes because of the injustices we were forced to suffer after Oklahoma became the 46th state in 1907. The first large party of black settlers arrived in northern Alberta in the spring of 1908, seeking that illusive freedom that always seemed to be just a little beyond their reach.

Blacks who lived in Alberta before this wave of immigration were few. In 1901 only 37 black settlers lived in Alberta, including the most famous of all, John Ware, a cowboy and rodeo hero who ranched in the Calgary district before 1890. Others were Ben Washington, who lived in High Prairie, and a Mr. Bond who served with the North-West Mounted Police at Fort Macleod.

Many of the black immigrants to Canada would have liked to stay in Oklahoma (indeed, a large number returned after experiencing Alberta's biting cold winters), but the venom of racism was too bitter for many to swallow. Even though blacks made up a significant percent of the population of Oklahoma, they were not accepted on equal terms; and after statehood, their status became intolerable. We can better understand the black plight in Oklahoma if we look back some 75 years.

The United States Congress in 1828 designated most of what is now the state of Oklahoma as Indian Territory, and the government reserved much of the area for tribes from the Southeastern U.S. at a time when restless, land-hungry Americans were spreading relentlessly westward in search of free land. The government ordered all whites in the area to leave.

This might appear at first glance to have been a kind act on the part of the U.S. government, but it wasn't. The government had strong ulterior motives. By the 1820s, Southern Congressmen faced heavy pressure from their white aristocratic constituents to remove the Five Civilized tribes—the Choctaws, Cherokees, Creeks, Seminoles, and Chickasaws—from the Southeastern U.S. to free up lands for the advancing cotton frontier so that white land owners might expand their holdings.

With the invention of the cotton gin, cotton became a profitable venture; but it also created a need for what was becoming increasingly valuable land. White farmers (later referred to as plantation owners) could become wealthy by producing cotton with slave labour and selling it to New Englanders or to the British for the manufacture of textiles.

But Southeastern Indian tribes were already producing cotton to a much larger extent than some historians previously assumed. They too owned black slaves and it was the slaves who were forced to till the soil, carry out domestic chores, plant and harvest crops, and perform other duties for their Native American masters.

For years Indians and their slaves had lived undisturbed, but that changed when the United States adopted a removal policy in 1830. The Five Civilized Tribes stood in the way of white ambitions, and so they would have to go, leaving their ancestral homes where they had grown crops, reared families, and created a culture.

To the U.S. government, this seemed an ideal solution to the Indian problem. Indians could be removed from the rich and valuable lands coveted by whites, while white conscience could be assuaged by replacing the homes the Indians had lost with lands that would be exclusively their own. Never mind that Indian Territory was believed to be undesirable for white settlement, filled as it was with hostile indigenous Indians and Spanish intrigue. It was also an area mislabeled by early explorers as the American desert, similar to the mislabeling of part of the Canadian prairies—the Palliser Triangle—supposed to be worthless for agricultural development.

The removal of both the Indians and their slaves created incredible hardships and heartaches. Slave and master alike suffered in that terrible trek that became known as the "Trail of Tears," ending in a place then designated by the federal government as Indian Country—later Oklahoma.

So while white settlers poured into Missouri and Arkansas, others of a different colour were forced by federal troops to resettle on unwanted reservations far from their homes. Force, not economic gain, drove them from the tribal lands they had occupied for generations.

The government promised that the area designated for the Indians would be a "Permanent Indian Frontier," safe from white incursions, far and away from white settlement. The "Permanent Indian Frontier" proved to be short-lived.

The Civil War in the U.S. brought emancipation for slaves north of the Mason-Dixon Line. In the Southern States emancipation came only after the Civil War, but it still did not bring former slaves real freedom. Southern whites soon put in place new legal and illegal ways to control them. They were subjected to segregation on public transportation, in restaurants, schools, and in almost every other place of business. By various means, they were also denied the right to vote. Protest against such treatment could prompt a visit from the Ku Klux Klan.

Some blacks remained where they had lived most of their lives and accepted their condition quietly. Others sought new horizons where they hoped to be free from prejudice and fear. Some headed to the industrial North; others joined the march west in search of cheap land and the hope of better conditions in Kansas and Oklahoma—conditions they believed they earned and deserved by their service and loyalty to the United States.

During the Civil War, black soldiers had played a significant part in achieving victory for the Union. Some of the black troops of the Tenth Cavalry later helped build the commissary at Fort Sill, Oklahoma. The success of black and white troops and military necessity made certain the emancipation of blacks not only in the South but in Indian Territory as well. The only up-side to the issue of slavery in Indian Territory was that it was less harsh than in the American South. Here slaves were treated more like farmhands or domestic servants. Although President Abraham Lincoln issued the Emancipation Proclamation in 1863, slavery did not effectively end in the territory until three years later.

Chapter 2
Oklahoma

Again the Indians stood in the way of "progress." In the spring of 1866, federal officials and representatives of the Five Civilized Tribes met at Fort Smith, Arkansas, to hammer out details of a peace treaty and to sign reconstruction treaties. The government argued that the Indians had sided with the Confederacy and should be punished. This enabled the federal government to trump up charges of treason as an excuse to take their lands. In truth, the Indians had actually been split in their allegiance between North and South.

The federal government made the tribes sign a treaty that forced them to surrender a large part of their territory for the settlement of other Indians and required them to grant their former slaves allotments of land and accept them as full-fledged members of their tribes. This cleared the way for the establishment of the "Small Reservation" system.

The government's efforts to provide newly freed blacks a means of earning a living by ensuring them land was important. It helped to lessen the poverty experienced by blacks in many parts of the Deep South. Had the U.S. government adopted a similar policy for the rest of the nation after the Civil War, subsequent relationships between the races might have been better.

Some Indians, of course, balked at the idea of giving ex-slaves parcels of land, but eventually most blacks received an allotment of between 40 to 160 acres. Choctaws and Chickasaws preferred the removal of blacks from within their domain, and the latter ultimately refused to accept blacks as full-fledged members of their tribe.

Those blacks that became members of various Indian tribes made every attempt to assimilate and were, to some extent, successful with the Creeks. Some inter-married and black children attended government-run Indian schools. Others grouped together to form a number of totally black communities. In spite of the close ties with the Indians, they were never fully accepted as equals.

A hope began to brew among blacks for a territory that would be exclusively theirs. But that dream was not in their stars. Following a railroad boom that spread a web of tracks across the continent, a constant flow of pioneers spilled into the Northwest and Southwest. Further west lay arid or desert lands considered unfit for farming. Lying between these areas and occupied by Indians and blacks was Indian Territory with millions of acres of good soil. Lands that not long before held no interest for white settlers, now became the West's "finest garden spot wasted on Indians." Why not open it up for settlement so that hardworking farmers could transfer this wasteland into productive farms?

The thought soon found substance as thousands of lawless intruders swarmed into Indian Territory. The Creeks and Seminoles had held two million acres of rich land that the U.S. had previously ceded to them. But in 1879 it lay under siege. In Kansas, pioneers grouped around campfires discussing "Oklahoma District" with its mild climate, crystalline streams, and fertile soil. Railroad advertising whetted the appetites of the would-be holders of rich farm estates. Newspapers denounced the government for barring honest settlers from such an

"Eden." This further excited the homeseekers, many of whom took matters into their own hands and entered the forbidden territory. This was followed by larger and more organized incursions. The westward movement and its "manifest destiny" would not be stopped.

American soldiers were stationed at sites along the border of Oklahoma Territory to keep out intruders. This included a unit of blacks called Buffalo Soldiers. But all of their efforts could not hold back the flood of "Boomers" pressing at the gate. Ironically, fifty years later, many of the descendants of the "Boomers" would be fleeing Oklahoma (then a dust bowl) for California with their half-naked kids and mattresses stacked on top of broken-down jalopies in a "Grapes of Wrath" journey of despair.

Constant pressure finally succeeded and the Boomers won the day. As in the past, lawless action culminated in the U.S. government's changing Indian policy to the Indians' detriment; and the "Permanent Indian Frontier," was no more. It ended with a rush of pioneers (Oklahoma Boomers) into one of the nation's last public domains. In January 1889, President Benjamin Harrison opened a section of what is now Oklahoma to settlement and forced the Creeks and Seminoles to surrender their rights to the Oklahoma District for a little over $4 million. Two months later Congress opened the District to homesteaders and called the area "Unassigned Lands." The District would be thrown open at noon on April 22, giving rise to one of the most bizarre land rushes in the history of the world. Within hours nearly two million acres of Oklahoma District had been occupied. Scattered remnants of Indian tribes ended up living on 160-acre plots the government had allotted them. Many eventually lost that.

Blacks, principally from the South and from Kansas, also joined the land rush. The government permitted no discrimination against blacks at this time, and they were generally treated equally with the rest of those who would be taking part in the run. At the formation of Oklahoma Territory, blacks represented over 8 percent of the population—about 137,000.

Throughout the first decade of the twentieth century, more blacks entered Oklahoma and more than two dozen all-black towns were established, along with the increasing hope of an all-black state.

Molley and Crawford Hayes (parents of Floyd of whom we will hear later) and their family and George Ramsey and his family were among the first voluntary pioneers to head for Oklahoma and settle in what was then part of the Creek Nation. They left Mississippi in 1905 because of the frightful and hopeless conditions that prevailed there for blacks. When Oklahoma entered statehood, conditions for the blacks were similar to those that had driven them out of Mississippi. Not only were they subjected to the common prejudice and tyranny that they were forced to suffer in the Deep South but now they were also required to fence their land at a cost few blacks could afford. They were therefore forced to sell and move away for fear that their homes would be burned down. Their restless quest for freedom and opportunity would lead them to Alberta.

As increasing numbers of whites entered Oklahoma Territory, statehood became imminent; and segregation and racism became a greater concern among blacks. In 1906 the U.S. Congress passed the Enabling Act, paving the way for Indian Territory and Oklahoma Territory to become the state of Oklahoma. Segregation had for some time made strong inroads, and now there were efforts afoot to deny the blacks the right to vote after statehood. While the Enabling Act guaranteed all citizens the right to vote regardless of colour or previous conditions of servitude, segregationists found ways around the law to prevent blacks from exercising their rights.

The Enabling Act required the future state to hold a constitutional convention. Being properly represented at the convention was crucial for blacks, who were predominately Republicans as was Abraham Lincoln, the President who freed them. Blacks naturally turned to the Republican Party for help. The Democratic Party associated itself with segregation and white supremacy. They campaigned against the mixing of races and warned that the Republicans would promote such mixing. The most prominent topic of the campaign revolved around constitutional segregation. Whites were admonished to support the Democratic Party to avoid black domination.

The Democrats won all but twelve seats in the constitutional convention—an overwhelming affirmation that racism was alive and flourishing in the "promised land." The flood gates were now open to full-blown segregation following Jim Crow* traditions. Blacks however had one more card to play. They would lobby Republican President Theodore Roosevelt to veto any Jim Crow constitution. That failed when members of the Constitutional Convention omitted Jim Crow provisions in the constitution for fear that Roosevelt would indeed exercise his veto power. They agreed among themselves to wait until after statehood to apply segregation. The original constitution did, however, include provisions to

---

* Laws and attidudes discriminatory toward peoples of dark colour.

segregate schools and it gave the legislature powers to limit voting rights and to specify who was to be considered black.

In 1907, Oklahoma became a state. Instead of a black state, it became white and racist. Again blacks were subjected to intimidation and violence, especially when they wanted to vote. Soon, under the sponsorship of powerful southern Democrats, a "Grandfather Clause" in the state constitution eliminated almost all blacks from being eligible to vote. They were also singled out for menial labour, and schools were segregated. After statehood, the hated Jim Crow laws were enacted with their attendant burnings and lynchings. Slavery had been abolished but blacks still weren't free. They began casting about for alternatives.

William Buddy Robinson Jr. was the son of Mary Ellen and William Robinson Sr. They lived in Woodland, Mississippi, near Jackson. William Robinson Sr. had been granted a plantation. The white landowners liked him because he was "an obedient black." When he died, the land went to his son, William Buddy Robinson, born in 1875. William Buddy was young and aggressive with a mind of his own. White plantation owners didn't like him because they couldn't control him, so they planned to get rid of him and take his land.

A clan of the white plantation owners gathered together in the back of a store owned by one of its members to discuss ways to get rid of William Buddy. They decided to offer him $500 for his plantation. They were sure he would refuse the offer, so they would lynch him and take the plantation. The store owner, a friend of the late William Robinson Sr., didn't like the plan, so after the meeting, he slipped over to William Buddy's place and told him of the plan and advised William Buddy to take the money and get away with his family as fast as he could.

William Buddy had married Creola Aycock in 1892 when she was only 16. They had two children, Sharp and Loretta. William Buddy feared for their safety, so when the clan members offered him the money, he took it, much to their surprise. Wasting no time, he fled to Oklahoma with his family, including his mother Mary Ellen and his niece, Mary Chandler.

Years later his daughter, Hattie Robinson, visited the 160-acre plantation in Mississippi that had once belonged to the family. The white family who then owned the land and lived in a small frame house received Hatti as a welcome guest.

After living in Oklahoma for about five years William Buddy heard about homesteads in Alberta that could be obtained for a fee of $10. So he, his family (his wife Creole and their children, Loretta, Shawnee, Izora, Wilma Mae), his sister Hattie Robinson Sr. and her son Dempsy, Anne Robinson, the Gibson family, his mother Mary Ellen Robinson and her granddaughter Mary Chandler all boarded a train for Canada in 1910. Phyllis Day (Robinson), her family (Willis, Esther, and Hatcher) came a year later, arriving in Canada, December 25, 1911. While living in Edmonton Willis met Richard Funnell, a man from Keystone, who persuaded him to file on a homestead in the Keystone district. From this meeting the beginnings of the black settlement originated.

Chapter 3
Immigration to Alberta

It is not commonly known that many of the cowboys in the American West were blacks. Because the severe winter of 1885-86 was followed by the hot and dry summer of '86, the withered grass and dried up streams forced stockmen to drive their weakened herds north. During this time, fully one-fourth of all the American trail drivers from Texas to the northern ranges were black—a fact lost on Hollywood and American literature. Moreover, most were highly respected for their skills and bravery.

Some of the cattle were driven to the Crow Reservation in Montana and some as far as Alberta. Here was a land where a black might live free from prejudice and fear—a place of refuge far away from the many American whites who needed only a black face to launch them into fits of hatred. Some blacks stayed in Alberta. Obviously, most who settled there in the late nineteenth and early twentieth centuries were men.

For many blacks the word Canada had a magic ring. Early in its history, Canada had rejected slavery. In 1793, Upper Canada became the only British colony in North America to pass legislation abolishing slavery. On August 28, 1833, the British Parliament passed a law abolishing slavery in all British North American colonies. The law became effective on August 1, 1834.

Canada was a country of small family-run farms. These weren't the expansive plantations common in the southern U.S. to support slavery. Indeed, Canada was the termination point of the Underground Railroad that carried about 30,000 slaves to freedom. Blacks were greeted, accepted, and protected when they arrived in Canada. So, for Oklahoma blacks, maybe Canada was their promised land. Had not other persecuted people found refuge there? Mormon fugitives from Utah not only found sanctuary in Alberta but prosperity too.

It was a favorable time for blacks to look northward. Railways were being pushed west across Canada, and the vacuum through which they ran needed to be filled with sturdy settlers not only to make the railroads profitable but to create a presence to safeguard Canadian sovereignty against the pressures of land-hungry Americans. To fill this need, the Canadian government advertised for settlers and offered 160 acres of land to farmers who would settle in the West. In return, the homesteader would be required to pay a $10 registration fee, build a livable dwelling, clear a certain amount of land for crops in a given amount of time, and reside on the land at least six months out of each year.

Federal Minister of the Interior Sir Clifford Sifton probably did more than anyone to promote immigration to the Canadian prairies. He believed that promotion of immigration and settlement was a great national enterprise and that the government had both the right and the duty to pursue that end aggressively in a businesslike and systematic fashion to shape the country's future. Furthermore, he felt that movement to the prairies would stop without the constant promoting of the West.

Sifton held a clear vision of what constituted the desirable immigrant for the prairies. It was "a stalwart peasant in a sheep-skin coat born on the soil, whose forefathers have been farmers for ten generations, with a stout wife and a half-dozen children." He adhered to the theory that different races expressed different characteristics; and by applying this pseudo-science to immigration, he could settle the people on the land with the greatest chance of their succeeding and becoming prosperous. Therefore the promotion of selective immigration would be a good investment in Canada's future. His strong peasant stock, experienced in facing harsh elements characteristic of the prairies, could establish the farms on which their children and grandchildren would expand and make productive.

Conversely, there were those he believed who could not succeed. They were the Italians and other southern Europeans, Jews, Orientals, English city dwellers and, of course, blacks. He felt that these people, after an abortive attempt at farming, would gravitate to more populated areas and add to growing urban problems.

Canada traditionally favoured immigrants from Britain and areas of Western Europe. Eastern Europeans were also enticed to settle in the West because of their familiarity with farming in a climactic environment similar to what they would find on Canada's prairies. But Sifton's most dramatic change in seeking out immigrants for the prairies was the new emphasis he placed on convincing American farmers, especially those from the Midwest, to take up land on the prairies. By 1899, Sifton had more than 300 agents recruiting farmers to immigrate to Canada.

Sifton was proud of his efforts. "The exodus of Canadians to the United States has been stopped," he bragged. "Our agents are taking thousands of the best farmers of the western states and settling them upon our western prairies."

The Canadian government would eventually attract more than a half million American farmers. What never occurred to Canadian officials was that blacks, many of whom now looked to Canada as a favorable option, numbered among those farmers. That presented the government with a dilemma. The extensive promotion campaign with its exaggerated claims now had to be reversed where blacks were concerned. How could the government explain that the western prairies would be great for white farmers but not for black? How could the Canadian government exclude blacks from immigrating to Canada without offending the U.S. government? And if Canada did keep out blacks, what backlash could be expected from black voters living in eastern Canada? No, Canada could not through any kind of legislation exclude blacks from immigrating to Canada without dire consequences. It would have to be done in a subtle, surreptitious, and underhanded manner.

Canadian officials were directed to do all in their power to convince would-be black immigrants that Canada's climate was too harsh for them. This strategy experienced a certain amount of success. Many members of families that were considering the move to Canada were afraid to go to a country they knew very little about and many were afraid of the cold climate.

By 1910 Oklahoma's population included about 150,000 blacks, but their hopes for an all-black state had dimmed and died three years earlier with statehood.

Tension and apprehension increased. My mom and dad heard that there were more opportunities for blacks in Canada and less prejudice. This proved partially true. We encountered no legalized segregation or patterns of violence in Alberta, but neither did we find a haven of tolerance, and it wasn't long before it became abundantly clear that Canada did not want black settlers.

OKLAHOMA CITY, March 26.—The final action of the Canadian government in admitting to that country Negro families from Oklahoma is having the effect of further colonization movement among the Negroes, especially in Okfuskee, Muskogee and Creek counties, where there is a heavy Negro population and several exclusive Negro towns.

The first emigration *to* Canada during the past week was of ninety families, perhaps 500 Negroes in all, from Okfuskee county. They sold all their property in this state, intending to homestead quarter section claims in Canada. Many other Negroes are making preparations to start and indications are there will be a general exodus. It develops that the Canadian colonization work among the Negro has been in progress for several months, the intention being to move 1000 families, or about 7000 Negroes, this spring, of which the Clearview emigrants formed the advance guard. It is understood a treaty provision admits them to Canada if they have $5 [$50.00] each in cash.

The emigrants as a rule are educated Negroes, many of whom were taught in the government schools for Indians in old Indian Territory. They are leaving Oklahoma because of adverse legislation, "Jim Crow" coach and depot laws, the "grandfather clause" act that prohibits them from voting, separate school laws and others.

The Gazetteer and Guide, March 26, 1903

Chapter 4
Edmonton

Along with other black families, including the Robinsons, Baileys, Fords, Rosses, Proctors, Hayes (who later moved to Leduc, Alberta where they lived a year while building their home on their homestead in Keystone), our family took up residence in Edmonton around 1910-11.

Alex Ross, who came to Canada with his wife, six sons, and a daughter, was able to trace his lineage back to John Ross, the famous Cherokee Chief who stalwartly resisted U.S. seizure of 111,000 square kilometres of Indian lands in Georgia. Chief John Ross was a highly educated man—a graduate of Kingston Academy in Tennessee. He was also a patriotic American who fought under General Andrew Jackson (later President of the United States) during the Creek War in which the U.S. defeated the Creek Indians who had allied themselves with the British during the War of 1812. In spite of his services to his country and his people, his fight to reverse the Indian Removal Act (May 1830) fell on deaf ears. He was forced to lead his sedentary people from their communities of well-stocked farms, schools, and other institutions where they enjoyed a form of representative government to Oklahoma on an infamous journey known as the "Trail of Tears."

Some trudged through heavy snow in the dead of winter, often suffering temperatures below 0°F. Cholera and other diseases claimed the lives of many Indians and slaves alike.

Grandpa Ross, known as Daddy Bear, loaded box cars with oxen and other valuable possessions and led a pilgrimage to Western Canada from Oklahoma in 1910 or 1911.

Before the abolition of slavery, a senator for Virginia gathered up about one hundred slaves and led them to West Ohio where they received their freedom. Charles Proctor's great grandparents, who were part of that group, settled in Ohio. Charles was born in Wapakonsta. He later married Jesse Ross, the only living descendent of Daddy Bear, at Kamloops, British Columbia, in 1922. They came to Keystone district in 1924 and settled on a homestead about six miles north of Breton where they raised five children. Jesse, at the writing of this book, is ninety-five and in failing health.

The three Bailey brothers, Robert, Will, and Ben, came from Council Grove, Kansas, to Canada around 1910. Will brought his wife Matilda (Bartlett) and her mother from Dunlap, Kansas. Will and Matilda's son "Big Eddie" came with them. The climate was much too harsh for Matilda's mother, so she returned to Dunlap. The Baileys, Bartletts, and Hardings had left an area where the chief crops were wheat and sorghum.

The Bailey brothers left their parents and sisters behind in the States and took up temporary residence in Edmonton before moving to Keystone around 1911, where they all filed on homesteads, near each other. Ben, now settled, sent for his sweetheart, Mabel. When she arrived in Canada, they were married and moved onto their Keystone homestead.

A few years later Robert married Mary Chandler, who had come to Canada from Oklahoma with her family, the Robinsons.

Mom and Dad lived in Edmonton at this time. Dad found work in construction on the High Level Bridge. Its construction was a stupendous achievement that took three years to complete and cost $1 a rivet and the lives of three workers who fell to their deaths. On June 2, 1913, the bridge was officially opened and the first train crossed. "With the blowing and shrieking of many whistles and sirens, cheers from the scores of workmen employed on the bridge, and the hurrahs of the 200 or more passengers, the first train to cross the Saskatchewan River between Edmonton South and Edmonton North over the new High Level Bridge..." enthused the *Edmonton Journal.*

My sister Rosella was the first of our family to be born in Canada. Midwife Phyllis Day delivered her in our home in Edmonton.

Edmonton at that time centered around Jasper Avenue and 101st Street. The tallest buildings along Jasper Avenue were only three or four stories high. Campbell Furniture, North American Life Assurance, and the Hudson's Bay Company were close by. There were street cars, but no buses. Most of the black families lived around 97th and 101 Streets.

Edmonton was a rough, male-dominated city—a city where many women fell into prostitution, some out of desperation, others because that profession was one of the few open to women that offered financial opportunities. Young women, new to Edmonton, were particularly vulnerable. Women's groups did what they could to protect girls arriving in Edmonton. Through the

YWCA, booths were set up at the train station to meet incoming women new to Edmonton and escort them to decent quarters in which they could to spend the first few nights until they could establish themselves. The YWCA had renovated an old barn behind their building to serve as a special dormitory for young women to stay temporarily.

The city bustled with activity. The fur trade was still alive. Coal mines operated at full tilt, along with saw mills, lumber yards, and brick yards, mostly located in the river valley.

Jasper Avenue burgeoned with streetcars, horses, horseless carriages, and milling crowds on wooden sidewalks. It was noisy and riotous and teemed with gambling, drugs, prostitutes, and pimps. A 1912 survey reported that over a hundred brothels had been raided by police.

Unlike the warm receptions received by slaves arriving in Canada via the Underground Railway during the 1840s to the 1860s, blacks entering Edmonton received no such welcome. Their numbers living in Canada had never been large, but they had always been good, law-abiding, and productive citizens who came to Canada's defense in times of crisis.

During the War of 1812, black militiamen fought valiantly against American troops. Blacks were prominent in helping to subdue the Rebellion of 1837. In Chatham, Upper Canada, the Second Coloured Company of Chatham formed to fight against the rebellion started by William Lyon Mackenzie. Within a month of the revolt's beginning, about a thousand blacks had volunteered for service. They guarded bridges, buildings, and forts and took part in capturing rebel ships. Later, when the Fennians (forces of Irish descent from the U.S.)

made several raids into Canada, blacks helped defeat and drive them back to the U.S.

For a period during the 1860s, the Black Pioneer Rifle Corps, largely self-financed, served as the only armed force protecting Vancouver Island. They were among a group of blacks who arrived on Vancouver Island on the ship *Commodore*. They were freemen who came to Vancouver Island from California to escape the persecution they suffered there and to seek refuge under the British flag, which they associated with the abolition of slavery. Governor James Douglas welcomed them, and the black immigrants merged into the population and contributed generously to the Island's development.

Not only did they make up the Black Pioneer Rifle Corps, but many of them were persons of substance and good education. Peter Lester and Mifflin Gibbs were blacks who established one of the leading mercantile houses in 1858. Others immersed themselves in other businesses. They were English-speaking Christians who became active members of the local churches and practiced the middle-class social norms of the Victorian age.

But in Alberta in the early 1900s, all that faded into insignificance when the American stereotype of the black became deeply ingrained in the Canadian psyche. The American popular culture, which had a strong and growing impact on Alberta, gave birth and nurtured many of these stereotypes. After all, tens of thousands of American farmers streamed into Alberta to homestead. They did not leave life-long prejudices at the border.

It is amazing how a small number of black families, wanting only to mind their own business, make a living, and live in peace and freedom, could strike such fear and animosity in a white population, even though whites remained overwhelmingly in the majority. But afraid of us they were, even those who were well educated and in positions of power.

Frank Oliver was one of them and served well as a conduit through which the fears and bigotry of the time flowed. An Edmonton pioneer, he founded the Edmonton *Bulletin* in 1880 and published it until 1923. He was also a politician and eventually sat in the House of Commons in Sir Wilfrid Laurier's Liberal government. The coveted position of Minister of the Interior and Superintendent of Indian Affairs became his when Clifford Sifton stepped down. Oliver was just the person Edmonton needed to oppose black emigration. He aimed his attacks not only against blacks but also against other groups that did not fit into his white Western European preference. In his *Bulletin* he described Ukrainians (Galicians), who were settling in Alberta and other prairie provinces at the invitation of Clifford Sifton when he was Minister of the Interior as "a servile, shiftless people ... the scum of other lands ... not a people who are wanted in this country at any price."

Yet, Oliver wasn't averse to taking advantage of these people when it was in his best interests. During one election campaign, he is alleged to have sent his organizers out to visit Galician communities. They asked each Galician man whom he planned to vote for. If it was Oliver, he was told the correct day to vote—Monday. If not Oliver, he was told Wednesday—two days after the election.

Oliver had always been critical of his predecessor's policies, believing that emigration to Canada should be based more on a policy of racial selection. He argued that Sifton's encouragement of Galicians instead of British labourers would destroy Canada's national fabric. This was the person who now turned his efforts against black immigrants.

In Edmonton, protests against black settlement were most vociferous, and Oliver found himself under pressure to do something about it. Some newspapers reported that Edmonton had been targeted for a black "invasion" of immigrants, which prompted the Edmonton city council to demand the immediate segregation of all blacks.

The fears occasioned by blacks settling in Edmonton and its surrounding area were reflected in the statements and actions of several boards of trade in Edmonton and area, the Labour Council, and women's organizations. Newspapers got into the act and warned of the dire consequences to the country if black immigration were allowed to continue. It was a popular cause, good business, and it sold newspapers. To combat the Hun at the gate, discriminatory barriers were set up in Edmonton and Calgary, and petitions to Prime Minister Sir Wilfrid Laurier were circulated in major urban centers. The following is one example that appeared in the April 25, 1911, issue of the *Edmonton Capital* :

We, the undersigned residents of the city of Edmonton, respectfully urge upon your attention and upon that of the Government of which you are the head, the serious menace to the future welfare of a large portion of Western Canada, by reason of the alarming influx of negro settlers. This influx commenced about four years ago in a very small way, only four or five families coming in the first season, followed by thirty or forty families the next year. Last year several hundred negroes arrived in Edmonton and settled in surrounding territory. Already this season nearly three hundred have arrived; and the statement is made, both by these arrivals and by press dispatches, that these are but the advance guard of hosts to follow. We submit that the advent of such negroes as are now here was most unfortunate for the coun-

> try, and that further arrivals in large numbers would be dis-
> astrous. We cannot admit as any factors the argument that
> these people may be good farmers or good citizens. It is a
> matter of common knowledge that it has been proved in the
> United States that negroes and whites cannot live in proxim-
> ity without the occurrence of revolting lawlessness and the
> development of bitter race hatred, and that the most serious
> question facing the United States today is the negro problem
> ...There is not reason to believe that we have here a higher
> order of civilization, or that the introduction of a negro prob-
> lem here would have different results. We therefore respect-
> fully urge that such steps immediately be taken by the
> Government of Canada as will prevent any further immigra-
> tion of negroes into Western Canada.

Leading the opposition to black immigration was the Edmonton Board of Trade, an influential civic organization composed of the city's leading business and professional people. Other organizations jumped on the bandwagon. Boards of Trade at Strathcona, Fort Saskatchewan, Calgary, the Edmonton Trades and Labour Council, women's organizations such as the anglophile Imperial Order of the Daughters of the Empire (IODE), and the French-speaking village of Morinville endorsed Edmonton's petition. Out of a population of 25,000, more than 3,000 Edmontonians signed.

The IODE distributed their own petition that warned:

> ...the problem likely to arise with the establishment of these
> people in our thinly populated province must be plain to all
> and the experience of the United States should warn us to
> take action before the situation becomes complicated and be-
> fore the inevitable racial antipathies shall have sprung up.

A prominent Conservative from Lethbridge made his preference for a "white" Canada clear when he told a large audience in Edmonton that "We Want No Dark Spots in Alberta."

Newspaper editors marched in the vanguard of fear mongering over black settlements. They warned against "the invasion of Negroes." One Toronto newspaper rose the specter of race riots if more blacks were allowed into the country.

Resolutions, petitions, and editorials flew in all directions while a small number of blacks bent their backs to the heavy tasks of breaking the land and making a living.

And what was the big flap about?

There was always that fear of importing the racial problems experienced in the United States. Economics played an important part in releasing fears and then hatred. Would blacks not discourage white settlement and drive down the value of property? Would not black men work for less wages than white men and therefore drive down the standard of living? And then, of course, there was the sexual threat—the idea that somehow black men had an uncontrollable desire to seduce white women. IODE women were not reticent in expressing their fears on that account:

> We do not wish that the fair fame of western Canada should be sullied with the shadow of lynch law, but we have no guarantee that our women will be safer in their scattered homesteads than white women in other countries with a Negro population.

After hearing that 5000 more blacks from the American mid-West would be seeking admission to Canada, Oliver's direction was clear. Blacks had to be discouraged from coming to Canada.

In 1910, Oliver dispatched an agent to Oklahoma to convince black leaders that coming to Canada would not be in their best interests and to report on the situation among blacks in Oklahoma. As might be expected, reports came back to Oliver that in black communities "laziness is abundant and seems to have put its hallmark everywhere," an observation that seemed to be in contradiction to another revealing that Oklahoma blacks possessed "wealth much greater than that of the white settlers in the State." The agent firmly advised that blacks be prevented from coming to Canada, arguing that "There is so much of the Indian blood (approximately one-third of the blacks that settled in Alberta were of mixed blood—Creek and Seminole) in the coloured man of Oklahoma, carrying with it all the evil traits of a life of rapine and murder, that it will not easily assimilate with agrarian life."

Oliver now made a concerted effort to discourage blacks. A black clergyman was hired to go to Oklahoma and preach against black migration. The Canadian government withheld information about Canada that was requested by blacks.

In one case blacks aboard the Great Northern coaches in St. Paul's Union Depot in Minnesota were detained by Canadian authorities, who made it clear that they were not wanted in Canada. But this group was determined not to be turned back. While they waited apprehensively in and about the small station, their children restlessly seeking diversion by running about and playing in the mud, one of the leaders of the group refused to be bullied; and he contacted the U.S. State Department. What followed came close to inciting an international incident. The State Department sent a wire to the American Consul General in Ottawa demanding to know if Canada could exclude an entry on the basis of colour. The answer of course was no.

There were no formal avenues to keep them out, and the federal Liberal government had no intentions of enacting legislation that would. It did not want to strain Canadian-American relations by an immigration policy that would discriminate against a segment of American citizenry. Moreover, the Liberal government of Laurier did not want to lose the overwhelming political support of Eastern blacks. Informal methods of exclusion would have to be employed.

No one in authority wanted his discrimination policy spelled out nor his hypocrisy clearly revealed. Canadians had often criticized the American government for its stand on slavery and its treatment of blacks. Canada's written policy guaranteed that any healthy applicant with $50 could enter the country as an immigrant.

After much ado, the Red Northern Special pulled out of St. Paul, Minnesota, and headed unhindered toward Emerson, Manitoba, the Canadian border point where another hurdle was being erected.

Like a military campaign, the immigration department rushed 11 of its staff, including several doctors, to Emerson to encounter the "black invasion." Normally, crossing the border into Canada required nothing more than a friendly cursory examination by immigration officials. But when the blacks arrived, they were greeted like the Hun trying to invade Vienna. They were detained for three days at Emerson's Immigration Centre while doctors examined them from head to toe for tuberculosis and other diseases, while other officials pried into their finances.

Those that entered were all healthy and had far more than the $50 minimum required. One was worth $40,000. Another carried $10,000 in cash on his person.

The others possessed cash or credit cheques of between $1000 and $3000. Most had with them farm equipment and livestock, not to mention years of farming experience.

The grueling examinations found nothing that could legally deny them entry into Canada, and all but three were finally allowed to proceed.

In the meantime, under the promptings of newspapers and politicians, the outcry against the blacks grew in intensity and began to spread throughout Canada.

The blacks arrived in Edmonton on March 25, 1911, but they did not settle on the land right away. Many of the men left their families in Edmonton and went to their homesteads to build homes and clear some land. As there were no roads, no railway and no towns, the men followed a bush trail out of Edmonton and then cut a road through the bush to their homesteads.

During the summer months, the men worked at clearing and building. A certain amount of land had to be cleared before a homesteader could get his deed. Often the women came out to help the men in the summer, but everyone went back to the city for the winter. There the men worked at different jobs, such as hauling coal or working in coal mines to make some money during the winter.

In the spring of 1911, the public outcry against the blacks became intense. Oliver answered the cry on May 11 by drafting an Order-in-Council to bar blacks from Canada for one year. For reasons previously stated and because an election was coming up, Prime Minister Laurier had the order dropped. He could not risk losing the significant black vote in Halifax and in southern Ontario.

While the Canadian government never sanctioned discrimination, it did set up obstacles that would discourage blacks from trying to enter the country with an informal exclusionary policy, and it did turn a blind eye to discriminatory practices on the part of organizations, local governments, and businesses.

There were hospitals that refused to accept blacks into nurses' training. Some landlords refused to rent to them. Blacks were often barred from dance halls, bars, swimming pools, skating rinks, and other private and public facilities. Residential segregation was common in the larger urban areas. Both Edmonton and Calgary had areas of predominantly black residences, but segregation seems to have been more common in Calgary than in Edmonton.

While segregation and racism were being practiced openly, Canada ignored the reality and continued to mouth the myth that every race was welcome. Privately, it supported exclusion. Even the Canadian Pacific Railroad cooperated with this policy by excluding blacks from enjoying the reduced rates on Western tours to which every white settler was entitled.

In the end the combined prejudices of politicians, immigration officials, the press, various upstanding organizations, and the public at large were extremely successful in keeping blacks out and the West "racially pure." In 1901, only 98 blacks lived on the prairies. By 1911, after the greatest influx of immigrants to the prairies, only 1524 were black, while fully 750,000 white American settlers entered Canada between those years.

Black settlement soon became a non-issue. The government moved swiftly and efficiently to eliminate it, while at the same time maintaining the perception that

Canada was open to all. What couldn't be hidden were the basic racist attitudes that existed throughout Alberta because they had been so publicly and vociferously recorded.

Certainly the blacks weren't the only people to suffer discrimination. Chinese and Japanese also experienced more than their share. Slavs didn't fare all that well either. But with them there was a difference. It was accepted that they could be assimilated, but it was their massive numbers that became a concern. But Chinese, Japanese, East Indian, and black immigrants were considered inferior, undesirable people and it was seriously questioned whether they should be allowed to come to Canada at all.

While it is true that discrimination did exist in Edmonton, not all Edmontonians were guilty of it. Discrimination came from a very vocal minority. While more than 3,000 people signed a petition to end black immigration, more than 21,000 did not sign it. After the initial panic, most people settled down and accepted the black immigrants as friends and neighbors. Throughout the following years, Edmonton usually proved itself a tolerant and accepting city.

Chapter 5
To the Homesteads

Most black settlers came to Canada in extended family groups—fathers, mothers, grandparents, brothers, sisters, cousins and their families. These groups stayed together and homesteaded land close to one another.

A large group stayed around Edmonton until their homes were built on their homesteads and then they dispersed, usually in covered wagons, to various black settlements like Campsie, Wildwood, Battleford, Amber Valley, and Keystone (Breton). These communities were far from populated areas.

At one time there were 52 black families in Keystone. The Keystone area was typical of the type of land black settlers sought. It had ample water, grass, and timber. Many of those from Oklahoma already had experience on wooded land and knew how to clear it. Blacks also sought isolation which made it possible for them to establish a black community, relatively free of conflict with whites. Most blacks wanted to form their own communities and rule them without interference. They wanted to live in communities free from prejudice and racial tension. There existed a strong sense of community because many of the settlers belonged to the same fraternal organizations in Oklahoma such as the

Masons and Oddfellows that had organized groups of immigrants. But it also imposed great hardships, economically and socially and due to hardships and cold weather, some returned to cities to seek employment while others returned to the U.S.

William Allen and his wife Mattie were among the first black settlers in Keystone and were most instrumental in forming that community. They arrived around 1910. William Allen had seen the area and liked it and felt it would be a perfect place for a black settlement. He returned to Oklahoma to persuade other blacks to come to Canada, arguing that homesteads could be obtained for each male over eighteen.

William Allen was highly respected in the black community. He was born in Georgia before the Civil War. After the war he went west and lived in Kansas, Oklahoma, and Utah. Wherever he went, he seemed to come into conflict with his white neighbors, and he would be forced to move on. He eventually decided to try Canada after a violent clash with eight Ku Klux Klansmen in Oklahoma. He knew that if he stayed in the United States he would either be killed or be forced to kill in self-defense.

Soon more black pioneers started moving into the area. They included the Ramseys, Baileys, Days, Kings, Stricklands, Rosses, Alexanders, Hayes.

Floyd Hayes came to Canada with his parents, Molly and Crawford, his sisters, their husbands and brothers,[*] nieces and nephews[**] whose parents had passed away.

---

[*] Rueben Dureal, Jasper and Sammy
[**] Robert and Lottie McClenan

They arrived in Edmonton March 25, 1911, during the time when opposition to black immigration was at its height in every quarter. They stayed in Edmonton for a short time before moving to Leduc where they resided temporarily while building their home in Keystone. By 1913 they were snugly installed on their homestead far from the boisterous denunciations in Edmonton.

Floyd took up land of his own and after a brief courtship married Elizabeth Murphy in 1922. Elizabeth was born in Chandler, Lincoln County, Oklahoma in 1906. She came to Canada by train in 1910 with her parents Mr. and Mrs. William Murphy and settled on a farm in Amber Valley near Athabasca.

Floyd and his wife worked very hard farming four quarters in summer. In winter Elizabeth was left with the chores while Floyd worked in the Benson sawmill. There were times in the winter when the family could afford to eat only one meal a day—and that a meager one. Their children eventually numbered 10.[*]

Floyd Hayes received title to his land in the early 1900s and it has remained in the family since. A lot of history, changes, and everyday experiences have passed, but with pride the family carried on this life style. Vant Hayes is the only descendent of the area's black pioneers who continues to live in the farming community.

In 1938 Floyd moved his family to B.C. where he passed away in 1940 a few months before they were to return to Alberta. Only Floyd's brothers, Dureal, who lives in Council Grove, and Reuben, in Edmonton, are now living. Floyd's family still owns the home place, which was homesteaded in 1918.

---

[*]Nelly, Adrean, Elizabeth, Beaty (now deceased), Luvern, Lloyd, Lugene, Orville, Cleveland, Vant.

John Strickland, his wife, and four children were also among the first blacks to settle in Keystone.

Charlie King Sr., his wife Matilda and their family* came to Keystone in 1911 from the county of Okmulgee, Oklahoma. Their possessions included four mules and bedding.

After arriving in Alberta, Charlie King Jr. moved on his homestead and lived in a small log house with a tar paper roof, like his neighbours. He later joined the United Farmers of Alberta (UFA). He became a firm believer, worker, and leader of this organization, which was first established in Edmonton in 1909 to promote interest in rural economic, social and political issues. Charlie and Emma attended many conventions and rallies. Charlie would eventually become president of the Breton Farmers Union of Alberta and hold that office for many years. He believed that cooperation among farmers would improve conditions for all farmers. He and other members worked hard to establish "Farmers' Day" as a recognized holiday in Alberta. It is still honored today with picnics and celebrations throughout Alberta's rural communities.

In spite of the many hours he spent in politics and community involvement, he remained an attentive farmer.

Emma aided Charlie in all his endeavors. She raised a large garden and canned vegetables, wild fruit and wild meat. She tried to make their home as comfortable

---

* John and Stella King and Charlie Jr. and Emma King, Ernest or Sam (latter married Mattie Phillips), John, Nellie, Willie Mae, Odessa, and husband Henry Brooks, Lucy and husband Dave Gist, and Iola the youngest.

as possible. Teachers at Funnell School often boarded in their home.

Because of Charlie's commitments to various causes, he often spent nights away from home. During these absences, Emma, after milking the cows, fastening the chicken house, bringing in wood, and doing other chores, would walk with her dog to her mother-in-law Matilda's house to spend the night. Emma affectionately called Matilda "Mamma Ding."

On one of these excursions, the dog came face to face with a bear and two cubs that had wandered onto the trail. Fearing for the safety of her cubs, the mother bear rushed the dog who made a beeline to Emma. Terror froze Emma in her tracks and all she could do was pray as bear and dog raced in circles around her trembling form. After what seemed an eternity, her prayers were answered when the excited cubs dashed into the bush with the mother bear fast on their heels. Breathing a sigh of relief she turned homeward on rubber legs and stayed there.

Emma spent a lot of time with her sister-in-law Iola Gist (Aunt Pic) and Mary Bailey, her best friend. Mary really enjoyed her life at Keystone. She always made her own bread. Her method of setting yeast was unique. She would set her yeast overnight wrapped in coats to keep it warm.

The three lived close together. In the winter they would take the sleigh and go from house to house visiting. There was always something to do. In summer they travelled by wagon to Yeoford for basic supplies—flour, salt, sugar, and other staples. It took all day to go the twelve miles. There were no roads because the land was mostly muskeg. On one occasion the trail was so bad because of a heavy rainfall that they had to tie the horses to a big tree and pull the wagon out of the muskeg themselves.

Charlie and Emma's home was a place where one could find warmth and hospitality. Often RCMP constables on their way from Yeoford where they were stationed stopped at their place and spent the night before travelling on to Berrymoor or Lindale. In the morning Charlie would use his team to take them to their destination, while the constables' team rested in the barn.

Emma and Charlie had no children of their own, but they took in other people's children from time to time.

They went back to Oklahoma once to visit, but things had changed so much that Charlie never again wanted to return. Emma, however, went back many times.

It's a long way from the sultry heat of Mississippi to the windswept expanses of Central Alberta. It seemed even longer when the winter winds whistled through the chinks in the log house that George Ramsey built in 1910 on his 160 acres near Keystone.

But to George it was heaven because he had a piece of earth to call his own and was free from the segregation and prejudice that prevailed in the U.S., despite the abolition of slavery. Times were hard then, but when you are free, hard times are easier to take. George farmed and later opened Keystone's first post office, three miles north of present-day Breton. He went to Yeoford on horseback once a week for the mail.

George wasn't the first to haul mail from Yeoford. That honour belongs to Sanford Nelson, a big charming man respected by everyone who knew him. He first operated a sawmill in 1907 in the neighboring community of Winfield; but when a dam project on the Saskatchewan River, for which he was sawing timber, fell through, he began carrying mail from Yeoford to Buck Lake. That was in 1911.

He later erected Nelson Hall on Breton's main street, where movies were shown on weekends. Many social events were held in the hall—basket socials, dances, and other activities. Many a young man spent three months' wages bidding on his sweetheart's basket.

George's son Rolla was 22 when he came to Alberta. He and Ophelia Hayes were married five years later in 1915 in Keystone.* In 1919 Rolla took over the operation of the post office.

The Benson brothers, Albin and Oscar, were in the area long before the first black pioneers moved in. They came to Alberta from Sweden in 1905, and each filed on adjoining homesteads. By the time the black pioneers moved in, the Benson brothers were operating a portable sawmill, which provided many of the settlers with much-needed work. They called their enterprise the Strawberry Sawmill Company. A planer was later added to the mill.

William Allen persuaded my dad, Sam Hooks, to file on a homestead in Keystone. In 1915 my dad filed on a 160-acre homestead with a creek running across it.

Shelter was the first concern for Dad, as it was for every homesteader. The houses homesteaders built were small log structures with tar paper roofs. Dad would go out to the homestead, usually in the summer, and work on building the house and clearing a plot for a garden.

---

* They had ten children--Ella, Mildred, Roy, Vi, Stella, Margaret, Ethel, Martha, Walter, and Phyllis.

Finally, the day came when Dad was ready to move the family to their new home. He and my brothers, Ellis and Elmer, piled the wagon high with our belongings and tied the horses and cattle securely to the wagon. Ellis and Elmer also helped Dad take care of the animals while on the trail.

There were no roads, and in some places there weren't even trails. The mules pulled the wagons over logs, stumps, and through bogs. Often mother and the kids had to get off the wagon and walk or help push it out of the mud or over fallen logs and stumps.

Mother loved the trees. Years later when she would reminisce about travelling along the trails, she would always remark, "The trees were beautiful. They seemed to reach right up to the sky."

The move took almost a week, so they camped along the way. Virginia was eleven or twelve, and she helped Mother with cooking and looking after Rosella, the baby, who was then only two years old. I had not yet made my grand appearance.

As they neared the Keystone area, the crude log shacks of other black homesteaders came into view. Most had only one room, although some of the larger families had two. The rooms were divided by curtains made of flour or sugar sacks sewn together. The furniture was largely what they had brought with them from the U.S. Many of the homesteaders made their own furniture out of slabs of rough lumber. That's what most of our family's furniture was made of, except for Mother's cherished oak table and chairs that she had brought from Oklahoma.

The outside walls were covered with mud mixed with straw. Sometimes a small amount of cow manure was added to make the mixture more adhesive. They mixed the mud, which they called "dabbing," with hoes and shovels until it was a smooth paste. Dabbing was put between the cracks in the logs to keep out the weather and insects. When the mud dried, it was as hard as cement.

The walls were often white washed with a solution of lime and water to produce a clean white effect. Some settlers covered the inside walls with gray or blue heavy wallpaper almost like tar paper, making the inside of the house look bright and cheery.

Roofs were covered with tar paper, and slabs were nailed at intervals to hold the tar paper down. After every strong windstorm or heavy rain, the roof had to be patched. High winds often tore the tar paper and blew pieces of it off the roof and into the trees. Then the roofs had to be repapered. Sometimes when it rained, pots and pails were distributed all over the floor to catch the water. "Sprinkling on the outside and raining on the inside" was a common phrase.

The floors were rough hewn logs. One had to be careful not to get slivers. The women made rugs out of old rags and gunny sacks to cover at least some of the floor.

Wood stoves heated the houses, and coal oil lamps provided light. Mail was brought from Yeoford on horseback. Yeoford was only about twelve miles away, but the trail was often strewn with fallen logs. In winter sleighs became the main mode of transportation. Before starting out on a winter excursion, Mom would heat up rocks in the wood stove and then wrap them in rags, making wonderful foot warmers. Then we would pile into the sleigh, cover ourselves with blankets, find space for our feet on the foot warmer, and slip onto the trail with the gentle hiss of runners on snow. If the weather turned ugly, we would have to stay the night at our destination and return home the following day.

When my family arrived at Keystone, only three white families lived in the area. Richard Funnell was an early settler who lived in a small log house with a sod roof.

Mr. Beaumont lived alone after his housekeeper left. Once he had a bear look in at him through his window. He calmly stepped outside and shot the intruder at point blank range with his shotgun. He could have avoided the danger of being mauled by the bear by shooting it through the window; but he explained, "I didn't want to break the glass."

The Fleshers were white folks too. They came after we did and were a welcome addition to the community. James Flesher, his wife Clara, and their three children came from Terra Haute, Indiana, to Carmangay, southern Alberta in 1911. While there, Mrs. Flesher took patients into her home to nurse. They were sent to her by a local doctor. Most were maternity patients, and she became very skilled at bringing babies into the world.

From Carmangay they moved to Keystone where they bought the Ricker Ranch, the site of a large logging operation.

Clara served the community as a midwife. She brought Kathryn, Richard, me, and Beatrice into the world in that order. She was always a busy woman who loved making rugs and quilts in her spare time. She passed away in 1956 at 85.

The government paid the settlers to "prove up" on their homesteads. They were given a certain number of years to have thirty acres plowed.

Overall, homesteading proved a daunting task; in the Keystone area it was almost impossible. Not only did homes have to be built out of the wilderness but the land had to be cleared and prepared for crops with axes and grub hoes. Spruce stumps as large as a metre in diameter had to be wrestled from the unyielding grey-wooded soil.

Due to wet weather and the hardships of clearing and breaking land, Rolla Ramsey was unable to get his thirty acres under cultivation. So when he heard that the government man was coming to be pay him a visit, he plowed a furrow around thirty acres of land so that when he was asked how much land was broken, he could truthfully say he had plowed "around thirty acres of land."

Later the requirements for "proving up" were increased. Each homestead was required to have at least ten head of cattle to qualify. Well, most homesteaders had only one milk cow, so when the government inspector was expected at a certain homestead, several farmers would get together and put all their cattle on the one farm so the farmer would be able to point to ten head of cattle and meet the government qualification.

The inspector soon caught on, however, and told them to start marking their cows, as he was tired of coming out to look at the same ten head of cattle every time a settler wished to qualify for "proving up."

The blacks had established a close-knit and friendly community, much admired and respected by neighboring communities. In the March 25, 1914, issue of the *Strawberry Plaindealer*, published in Telfordville, Alberta, Aubrey Bray described the Keystone area as consisting of "mostly blacks" where great vegetables, oats, and barley are grown. He described the people as hospitable and their homes as being tidy and clean with brightly coloured carpets, knick knacks, and polished furniture, "giving the interior of the house an almost suburban appearance.

Chapter 6
Living Off the Land

The first cabin Dad built was made of logs near the creek running across our quarter section. It measured about 12 by 18 feet. He built part of the cabin into the bank of the ravine, and earth was banked around the outside of it to deflect the wind, snow and cold.

The windows were at ground level. One had to descend three steps from ground level to enter. The roof was covered with the customary tar paper and slabs. Flour sack curtains divided the inside of the cabin into four rooms. The boys occupied one small bedroom and the girls another. Mom and Dad had a bedroom, and the fourth room was the kitchen. As the family increased, Dad added more rooms.

The kitchen contained a wood-burning cook stove with a reservoir and a tall heater. We heated the house with wood—a plentiful and free source of energy. Then, of course, sitting prominently in the centre of the room was Mom's treasured oak table and chairs that she had brought from Oklahoma. Winters were bitterly cold and the snow was deep. The settlers were not used to this type of weather. I can remember my father-in-law, Willis Day saying, "We bought winter clothes before leaving Oklahoma, but they were not warm enough for the Canadian winters. It was December when we reached Winnipeg and it was so cold we had to look down to see if we had any clothes on at all."

The settlers had no winter footwear. When they went outside, they wrapped their feet in gunny sacks to keep them warm. The children did the same when they went to school in winter.

Thick bush and tall trees surrounded our house. The entire area was covered with heavy bush except for a few cleared acres and, of course, vegetable gardens which every settler depended upon. Very little money ever passed hands. Most settlers lived off the land and bartered when a need arose.

There were about 150-200 black people living in the area. They lived a free life and didn't have to get up to go to work. They stuck together. It was impossible to live independently because it was very hard to make a living.

Loggers made between $1 and $3 a day contracting. While trying to "prove up" on their homesteads, some settlers made a bit of money hauling lumber by mule team to Leduc or Edmonton, where they received $5 to $6 per load or they traded lumber for groceries, clothing, or farm equipment. Of course, in those days the pioneers had their own chickens, pigs, and milk cows.

Money being scarce, men from Keystone usually worked in Edmonton to get money for supplies. The closest town to Keystone when the blacks first settled there was Leduc, fifty miles away. It was a four-day round trip by horse team. If the weather proved contrary, it would take a week or more to get there and back. Spring was the worst time to travel. A thick gumbo sucked up everything, making travel all but impossible. The first stop out of Keystone was Stone's Corner, just east of Warburg. Travellers usually spent the first night there.

Alfred Stone was born in Ontario and came to Alberta around 1908. He and his wife Pauline homesteaded in what is today the Warburg area. They opened a post office named Stone's Corner in the spring of 1909. Alfred served as post master and hauled mail from Telfordsville. He also operated a small sawmill and raised six children.

Settlers from Keystone on their way to Leduc would stay an Stone's Corner overnight and try to complete the journey to Leduc on the following day. They always carried their own bedding and feed for their horses. Stone was always pleased to put weary travellers in his barn loft at no charge. If for any reason the travellers couldn't reach Leduc from Stone's Corner, they could stop over at Buford, about 12 miles west of Leduc.

A trip to Leduc was always a major undertaking, but it was the closest place to store up on the necessities they could not provide for themselves such as flour, sugar, salt, clothing, etc. When the Yeoford store opened, it was much more convenient, but a trip there could still eat up a whole day. At that time you could buy butter for 10 cents a pound and eggs for 5 cents a dozen.

Most of our consumer goods were locally produced. Land was cleared for fields or gardens in areas burnt over by fire or less densely covered with bush. All of the settlers had a few cows and chickens. The women, with the help of the children, tended large gardens, the produce of which supplied the community with their main source of food. The women also canned vegetables and wild berries, which grew like weeds throughout the bush.

After school, we children worked in the garden or did such chores as bringing in the night supply of wood. The older children split wood and made kindling for the next day. Weekends and holidays were spent in this fashion. Children also toiled hard in the fields, pulling roots and cutting brush with an ax. Women and children usually did these jobs because the men worked away from home to get money for other needed staples and supplies.

But they enjoyed berry picking, and there was a vast number of different types of wild berries including strawberries, blueberries, saskatoons, gooseberries, black currants, red currants, pincherries, chokecherries, three different kinds of cranberries, and others with names we didn't know. There were edible greens, mushrooms, and dandelions that made excellent wine.

After exhausting all the berries on their land, Elizabeth Hayes would ask other farmers if she and her children could pick pigeon berries on their farms. They always gave their permission with the stipulation that she not take the blueberries. She would agree, but often the sight of blueberries was too much of a temptation and she would secretly take a few and hide them under the pigeon berries.

Everyone was an expert on root cellars for storing vegetables, and each family had a unique way of constructing theirs. Our root cellar was made of logs and dug into the side of the creek bank. It faced south and was about five feet high and five feet wide. A vent protruded from the south wall. Bins were made for the vegetables—potatoes, carrots, beets, turnips, and parsnips. These were covered with straw in the winter.

Because our meals were mostly home-grown, they always had the taste and texture of home-grown food—new vegetables, prairie chicken, rabbit, or tame chicken. My sister Vergie's kids remember how they used to look forward to family gatherings at Grandma's. Her meal preparation was an art form that she nurtured throughout her life. Everything was so basic, yet everything an adventure. The crowning climax of every visit for the kids was when Uncle Edward would take them down to the ravine to chop ice for homemade ice cream.

Ours was a subsistence economy; therefore, the men and some of the women in the community hunted. After all, we lived in virgin wilderness and sometimes, when our larders were low, we hunted out of season. Indians could hunt out of season; and at least in the States, we were considered Indians and the Canadian government representatives themselves referred to us as Indians on occasions. However we looked at it though, hunting out of season just wasn't right, and sometimes we got caught.

Wild animals such as deer, wild chicken, prairie chicken, rabbits, bears, groundhogs, and moose were plentiful. There was the ever-present porcupine, but it was unlawful to kill it because it could be used as food for travellers who were either lost or out of food in the wilderness. The existence of porcupines saved many lives because they're so easy to kill. I never ate a porcupine, but I'm told they taste something like pork.

The animals never bothered anyone unless they themselves were bothered. They would attack to defend their young. Most men went hunting, so we always had plenty of wild meat. Because of the abundance of berries, bears were a common sight.

My two older brothers actually domesticated a deer. It was just an orphan fawn when they found it. He became part of the family and followed my brothers all over the property. He used to wrestle with the kids and would come into the house looking for cake, bread, and other food. My brothers put a bell around its neck so that they could keep track of him as he grew older and wandered farther afield. Then one day, he didn't come home and we never saw him again. We were a sad lot for a long time because we had all grown to love that beautiful and gentle creature. Hunters probably killed him. Being tame, he would have made an easy mark.

Occasionally we'd spot the odd pack of wolves. They never attacked anyone to my knowledge, but they could give settlers a terrible fright.

My older sister Vergie told of an incident in the early '20s. Looking out the window one day, she spotted nine wolves approaching the house. Locking the door, she warned the rest of the household of the approaching unwelcome visitors, and a frightful hush fell over the house as they peeped out of the windows and watched the wolves slink passively past the cabin and disappear into the bush.

Like any community, we had our ups and downs and our own memorable local adventures. One day my brother Richard and I were going to get milk from Walter Johnson, our neighbor. We went down the hill and across the creek where we had a garden and a large potato patch surrounded by two barb wire fences to keep the cows and horses out. Richard and I were smoking cigarettes we had stolen from Dad. It was dusk and in the distance we could hear talking and laughing. We thought it was our older sisters coming home from our brother Ellis's place.

We could not let them see us smoking or we'd be in deep trouble. Richard and I threw the cigarettes away and ran like jack rabbits across the field. I got through one fence, but forgot about the other and hit it at a dead run. A barb tore my cheek right through to my gums.

Well, we had to go home. I was bleeding like a stuck pig. My hands and mouth were full of blood. Mother was so excited she didn't even ask why we were running. She finally got the bleeding stopped and bandaged me up. I still have the scar to remind me of that little episode many years ago.

My grandmother didn't like Canada, so she went back to Oklahoma before I was born; therefore, I never knew my grandparents, aunts, uncles, or cousins. My parents were too poor to go back to Oklahoma; fortunately, they stayed and raised ten children—all proud Canadians.

My dad was away working a lot. He worked in the coal mines in winter and in the summer in Edmonton, so Mother was home alone a lot.

At first our family group was small, and I often felt as though I had been cheated because the other children I knew had many cousins, grandparents, uncles, and aunts. We did have one aunt that came to Canada—Aunt Leola Allen—but she and her husband settled in Campsie. Our family went to visit them once when I was very small. I don't know where they are now because Mother never heard from her again.

Campsie was covered with timber that attracted many sawmills and offered employment to early settlers. It had a store and a post office. Between 1914 and 1935, Mr. Beaver, a black pioneer, ran the Campsie post office. The store was a 20 by 30 foot log building. They had rice and beans in barrels. Once or twice a year they would get oranges and bananas. There was a big box heater in the middle of the store where people would sit around and gossip and tell yarns about their experiences.

There were no roads to Campsie, only trails that weaved through swamps and muskeg. Some of the timber had been burnt over and rotting logs were strewn at various places on the trail. You could walk two blocks on logs and never touch the ground. There were only forty black settlers in Campsie, not enough for the black pioneers to run a successful business of their own.

In the early years of the Keystone settlement, doctors, nurses, and medicine were nonexistent. Fortunately, most of the people remained healthy. We had clean fresh air, free from the chemical contaminants of industry and the automobile. Our water was pristine. Our food was fresh and free of additives. We never worried about fiber in our food. Everything we ate had fiber. Our life was not easy, but it was simple and healthy.

The settlers had to improvise their own health care, and they depended on home remedies. Mom possessed a broad knowledge of cures for illness or injury. Most of it was the product of the rich folklore she grew up with when living among the Creek Indians in Oklahoma. She used herbs that grew wild such as dandelions and nettles. Willow bark and twigs served as an excellent remedy for pain. She made poultices from rabbit droppings, which she applied to the chest for various respiratory illnesses. As children, we gathered peppermint, which grew abundantly in the ravine. Mother dried it and we drank peppermint tea in the winter for colds. We also drank hot lemon tea and mother would rub Mentholatum on our chests when we had the flu. Cough syrup was made from a mixture of honey, lemons and grapefruit. In the spring, we ate dandelion, pigweed, and nettles as greens.

Another source of curing colds came from our lamps. Before there were gas lamps, everyone burned coal oil. A couple of drops of coal oil or turpentine put on sugar was used as a cold remedy. (When the coal oil can was filled at the store, the storekeeper put gum drops on the spout to keep the coal oil from running out. We children always argued over the gumdrops.) Goose grease was rubbed on the chest and back and then mustard plasters were applied as a cure for chest colds. Poultices made with hot cornmeal and mustard were used to fight the cold bug. If the mustard was too strong, it could actually blister you. My wife told me that when she had whooping cough, she was given mare's milk. Carbuncles were treated by applying linseed meal dampened with warm water to the carbuncle until it came to a head. Then cold bread was soaked in sweet milk and applied to the carbuncle until it drew the core out.

They rubbed dirt and I think spider webs on insect bites to stop the itching. I don't know what kind of dirt they used, but it must have worked. Most people, especially the children, wore asafetida* around their necks. It's like a rock that smells terrible. Almost everyone wore it during the flu epidemic of 1918.

There were some things that home remedies couldn't cure. In her early twenties my oldest sister Virginia suffered an appendicitis attack. My brothers Ellis and Elmer walked to Stone's Corner to borrow a car to take

---

* The fetid gum resin of various oriental plants of the carrot family formerly used in medicine as an antispasmodic and in folk medicine as a general prophylactic against disease—*Webster's Ninth Collegiate Dictionary*, 1983.

her to the hospital in Edmonton. They returned home, loaded my sister into the car, and set off for Edmonton. Mother couldn't go with them. She had to stay home with the other children, but I can remember her saying how worried she was. She prayed all night.

The car broke down on the way, and they were forced to spend the night on the road. All the time my sister was writhing in pain. The next morning they repaired the car and rushed to Leduc to catch a train to Edmonton. We made it, but it was a close call. We almost lost her. Luckily, Virginia's extraordinary health and strength pulled her through a torturous ordeal.

However healthy the black settlers were, like everyone else, death would inevitably come a-callin' now and then, and so the settlers were in need of a cemetery. Unable to agree on where to put it, they finally decided that the first family to lose a member would donate the land for the cemetery. They felt it should be near the road, but no one knew where the main road would eventually be built. In 1910 the first death occurred in Harry Allen's family, and they donated a cemetery plot on the southeast corner of their land.

Years later when my wife and I went to get the title for the cemetery, it was not listed in the Lands Title Office. Records had not been kept. They had not been sent to the Registration Office of Deaths and Births, so when the Breton and District Historical Society (of which my wife Gwen was president and I was on the Board of Directors) decided to restore the cemetery in honor of our black pioneers, some names could not be found.

The Historical Society repaired and rebuilt the fence and erected a cairn on which there were listed twenty names on a plaque. There were others buried there, but those listed were all we could find.

We buried a small time capsule under the cairn with instructions for it to be opened in a hundred years. The instructions are kept in the Breton Municipal Library. The capsule contains a dollar bill, a copy of the local newspaper, *The Western Representative,* and a copy of the *Ladder of Time,* a Breton and district history book.

Over the years the graves were covered with colored glass broken into small pieces, probably to keep wild animals from digging up the graves.

As the population grew, more white settlers came from different parts of the world and took up homesteads. With the influx of white settlers, especially those from the States, racism emerged. The whites did not want to be buried with the black settlers, so they built their own cemetery in 1920.

The Keystone Cemetery was declared inactive after Emma King was buried there in 1983. The following quote appeared in a local newspaper:

> Keystone, the black Pioneer Cemetery, a symbol of the region's history—just north of Breton stands a silent testament to about fifty black families who were predominately the first to populate the area early this century. To my knowledge, there are only three or four such cemeteries in Alberta.

Inspired by their courage and tenacity, my wife wrote this poem to honour their memory:

OUR PIONEERS

The Black Pioneers to a new land came,
Around the year of nineteen ten,
Oklahoma and Kansas they left behind
A strange new life to begin.

They left a country so warm and rich,
With fruit plus nuts and grain,
They chose Alberta that was rugged and cold,
Huge trees covered the rough terrain.

In this new country they could purchase land,
For every man and grown up son,
With ten dollars they filed on homesteads
But their hard work had just begun.

The winters were cold their clothes were light,
They did not give up in defeat
They could not buy boots to keep out the snow,
So wrapped sacks around their feet.

They built tar-papered shacks close to a creek,
Cleared land for garden and grain,
Gathered wild berries and edible herbs
To prepare for snow and rain.

Fierce wolves howled at night
Filling them with fright,
Wild animals lurked very near,
The men would go hunting and often returned
With a hare, a moose, or a deer.

We say "Thanks" to these people who settled our land,
They worked hard and subdued all their fears,
May God bless them every one
Our Faithful Pioneers.

Chapter 7
Keystone

Among the first priorities Keystone's black community had to deal with was the establishment of the most basic institutions. First was an informal local government through which the community could make the necessary decisions affecting their lives. It was a loose form of government, having no real power. In fact, it wasn't really a government, but a committee dominated by the older and more influential members of the community.

Because the pioneers were strongly religious and had always gone to church in the States, the first institution to take form was the church. They felt an urgent need to worship God in this new land, and therefore everyone in the community took part in its planning and building. In September 1911, Good Hope Baptist Church, a little log building, held its first service. Its name was appropriate, because to succeed in the harsh environment the parishoners needed not only strength of will but also a heavy dose of hope. Our religion always gave us that.

Our little log church certainly was no great edifice, but it worked for us. It and its pastor were maintained by the free labour and products produced by its parishioners because there wasn't any money to speak of. One Sunday there were 51 people at the service and the collection plate yielded all of 82 cents. During good and bad times the church always served as the focal point of the community.

After the church came the need for a cemetery where we could lay our loved ones to rest; and finally a school to secure a prosperous and productive future for our children.

The Allens were active members in the Hope Baptist Church, which they helped to build. They served on the board and held the first church organizational meeting in their home on September 10, 1911. Charlie King Sr. chaired the meeting and Harry Allen served as secretary. The Allen family also helped build and operate Funnell School.

Charlie King was a very ambitious man, active in all community organizations. He assumed a leadership role in the construction of the Good Hope Baptist Church and the Funnell School and helped establish the Keystone Cemetery. He kept the records of the cemetery for many years and was secretary of the Good Hope Baptist Church. In 1918 he became secretary-treasurer of the Funnell School District, a position he held until 1954.

All of King's daughters served as secretaries of the Sunday school. Odessa King married Henry Brooks. He became the first reverend of the Good Hope Baptist Church and Odessa became Funnell School's second teacher. She taught my older sister and some of my brothers, but she never taught me. The first teacher was Victor Nordland, who began teaching in the one-room school in 1913, a year after it opened. He stayed only one year.

Rev. Henry Brooks became pastor of Shiloh Baptist Church in Edmonton from 1919 to 1920 and later

Neoma Hooks (Courtesy of Breton Museum)

Samuel Hooks (Courtesy of Breton Museum)

William Allen, the first black pioneer in Keystone, Alberta (Courtesy of Breton Museum).

Smith Boy (Courtesy of Nellie Whalen)

Virginia (Vergie), Mark's oldest sister (Courtesy of Gwen Hooks)

Mark Hooks (Courtesy of the Breton Museum)

Willard and Marg Robinson (Courtesy of the Robinsons)

Vant and Ethel Hays (Courtesy of Western Review, Drayton Valley)

KEYSTONE CEMETERY
1910 - 1983

MANY BLACK PIONEERS CAME TO ALBERTA
FROM THE U.S.A. IN THE EARLY 1900'S. THEY
FOUNDED GOOD HOPE BAPTIST MISSION AND
KEYSTONE CEMETERY.
WE DEDICATE THIS CAIRN TO THEM.

THOSE BURIED HERE ARE NAMED BELOW,
OUR APOLOGIES FOR THOSE WE HAVE MISSED.

ELSIE BRISCO	LARKIE FORD
DRUSILLA BRISCO	ZONA FORD
HARRY ALLEN	ALEX ROSS
BERTIE ALLEN	ERNIE ROSS
MARY PROCTOR	ABE BANNER
DOROTHY PROCTOR	JENNY BANNER
NORMAN PROCTOR	THOMAS SHAW
LEMUEL PROCTOR	BUS JONES
CHARLES PROCTOR	ANN TOSTON
JOHN BURTON SR.	MOLLY HAYES
JOHN BURTON JR.	MATILDA KING
IRWIN FORD	CHARLES KING
PRINCE FORD	EMMA KING
C. JEFFERIES	

BRETON & DISTRICT HISTORICAL SOCIETY

A VOTE OF THANKS IS OWED TO THESE PEOPLE FOR THE
HARDSHIPS THEY ENDURED IN THE OPENING OF A NEW LAND

REST IN PEACE

Plaque of Keystone cemetery

moved to the United States. They lived in the Keystone area for about eight years.

The Jones family came from Clearview, Oklahoma. Jesse's father came to Canada 1909, and Jesse, his mother, and sister followed in 1910.

Jesse's father hauled freight from Fort McMurray, Peace River, Grand Prairie and Athabasca. His mother did housework. Their combined income enabled them to keep their children in school.

Jesse never had the financial means to attend Normal School, but having completed high school qualified him to teach at Funnell School, where it was extremely difficult to get teachers. His classes contained from 32 to 44 students, ranging in age from 5 to nearly Jesse's age in grades 1 to 9. His teaching career at Funnell School continued from 1922 until 1927.

The school, a log building, was heated with a big potbellied stove that sat in the back of the room. There never seemed to be enough coal to keep the room warm in winter, even though in the summer men in the community would to go down to the creek and dig all the coal they wanted from the side of a hill. They would put it in the school yard and cover it up so that it wouldn't disintegrate. Wood was also stored for fuel. There were no storm windows, and the icy cold penetrated the large frosted shadeless window panes on both sides of the room and oozed through the many cracks in the walls. On cold winter mornings when the mercury dipped below zero, water and lunch pails were placed around the stove to keep them from freezing.

When it was too cold for the children to work at their desks, the teacher and class would crowd around the glowing stove, and soon there would be the aroma of burning wool from a sock that ventured too close to the fire.

In the warmth of the fire they would sing songs, especially Christmas songs. By the time the Christmas concert rolled around—the biggest event of the year, drawing people from miles around—everyone had learned quite a few songs. At one of the Christmas programs, the older girls danced to the Blue Skirt Waltz. How proud they were swirling around in their blue skirts. The school was so crowded that Santa had to enter through the window.

A crock of drinking water sat in one corner of the room and every student had his own cup which hung in an apple-box cupboard. Often the water was glazed over with ice. It came from a pump in the school yard, and students took turns filling the bucket when it was empty.

A cloak room, where students hung up their wraps and plotted mischief, was situated near the entrance. A box filled with wood occupied a space just outside the cloak room.

Jesse earned $75 a month. Out of that he paid $30 for room and board. Most of the rest went to take care of his mother in Edmonton. He often walked or ran home to Edmonton from Funnell on Friday after school and was back in his school room on Monday morning. Because there were no roads most of the way, Jesse didn't need to worry about traffic as he ran the trails toward Edmonton, but there was a lot of mud and muskeg to slosh through.

Addie Procter recalls school days at Funnell. She was so excited on her first day of school, even though she had to walk about three miles to get there. Sometimes in the winter when it was extremely cold, a neighbor who took her son to school in a cutter would stop and pick her up. How thankful she would be at such times.

When my wife Gwen started teaching at Funnell in 1946, the school and area were still very primitive.

During one winter Gwen started a hot lunch program that continued for years after. There was cocoa everyday except Wednesday when the students got hot soup. Everyone loved Mrs. Proctor's soup.

Willis and Matilda Day were prominent members of the Keystone community and the parents of my wife Gwen, their only child. Matilda had been widowed after the death of her first husband, Will Bailey. He died in the terrible flu epidemic that swept Western Canada in 1918. The epidemic also claimed the life of Tom Harding, another black pioneer.

Matilda was left with a child she and Will adopted and who was known affectionately as "Big Eddie." Matilda then married Willis Day in the Funnell School in 1919. My wife Gwen was the product of this marriage and was brought into the world in a rustic log house by her grandmother, Phyllis Day, a midwife who had brought many bouncing babies into the world. Gwen was not raised an only child. Her parents adopted three others later in life—Doreen, Keith, and Gerald.[*]

Gwen became a very creative person. She could work with her hands and her mind. That's probably why she was such a good teacher. To cite an example of her creativity, she once helped her mother improve a way to spin yarn by using a part of the cream separator.

---

[*] Doreen is married to Al Firth, and they have four children. Keith married Yvonne. and they have three children. Gerald married Pat. They also have three children. Their youngest son Bill was born on Willis' birthday and is named after his grandfather.

Willis sold his homestead at Keystone in 1922 and bought another farm in Radway, Alberta, next to the farm belonging to Matilda's sister. Ten years later he moved the family to New Brook, Alberta, where he bought another farm. Because of a number of crop failures, he was forced to sell out and the family moved to Edmonton in 1943, where Willis went to work at the Burns Packing Plant killing cattle. He had previously worked in that capacity at Swift's Packing Plant shortly after moving to Edmonton from Oklahoma. He was a hard worker and knew his profession. It wasn't long before he became head man on the killing floor.

Keystone was gone. Breton, which had become a predominantly white community had taken its place. But Willis never forgot his roots and dreamed of one day returning.

While working in Edmonton, he bought another farm near Breton. Shortly after Gwen and I married, Willis retired and he and Matilda moved onto their farm having come full circle. They lived there until they passed away, Matilda in 1969 and Willis in 1980.

Although Willis could not read or write, he had a terrific memory. He used to recite verbatim humorous prose at the many social events we used to attend.

Robert and Mary (Gwen's aunt) Chandler had three sons. Leslie, the oldest was born in Edmonton. Harvey and Eddie were born in Keystone. Mary's mother Phyllis Day was again the midwife.

Once when Leslie and Harvey were toddlers, the men folk went hunting ducks out of season. They told the boys they were hawks. One day the game warden came by and asked where their daddy was.

"Oh," they answered, "he's hunting hawks, the ones that swim on the lake."

Before leaving Keystone, Ben Bailey, Robert, and Phyllis Day, invested in a sawmill, but because there was no railroad in Keystone to transport their lumber, they moved the mill after a few months to Junkins (Wildwood).

They put a lot of sweat into that operation, and before long they had thousands of board feet of lumber ready for market. Ben Bailey was given the responsibility of taking the lumber to Edmonton to sell. Ordinarily Robert would have gone also, but illness confined him to his bed. So Ben had the lumber loaded on the train and took sole charge of the shipment to Edmonton.

He sold the lumber and, with a pocket full of cash, decided to see the sights of Edmonton before returning to Junkins. He was a happy-go-lucky guy who yielded easily to temptation and got drawn into a poker game. By the time he stopped laughing, he had lost all the money.

He couldn't go back to Junkins. Robert, as ill as he was, was left holding the bag and facing a lot of angry workmen that he couldn't pay. The lumber men had worked hard for their pay and were justifiably very angry when they learned that there would be none. They went on a rampage and shot up the mill and the horses. Then they destroyed the equipment, ending the Baileys' sawmill enterprise. Robert and his family didn't look back as they beat a hasty retreat by sleigh to Edmonton. They didn't have the money to afford any other means of transportation. Still extremely ill, Robert moved his family in with Mary's mother, Phyllis Day, in Edmonton.

Understandably, the Baileys never went back to Junkin or Keystone to live. After the sawmill disaster, they settled in Edmonton for good. Robert worked in the mines in the winter and for Crown Paving in the summer.

For the Bailey children, Edmonton, where they took their schooling, was a new world. They had been raised in predominantly black communities. Now they experienced life as a minority. Gwen Day, my future wife, stayed with the Baileys to finish high school, since there was no high school in Newbrook where her parents lived.

At Christmastime Harvey, Leslie, and Eddie Bailey were taken to see Santa Claus. They had never seen a white Santa Claus before. In Keystone, Charlie King Sr. had always played Santa Claus at the various events that took place around Christmas time and he was black. The boys were afraid of the new white Santa Claus until he started to hand out goodies. That broke the colour barrier for the boys who eagerly availed themselves of the tasty treats.

Harvey, who loved boxing, won the Western Canadian Featherweight Championship in 1935

As the years passed, more and more white settlers filtered into Keystone as more and more blacks left to work in towns and cities throughout Canada where there were more opportunities.

Once when asked why blacks began to drift away from the community they had themselves founded, Mary Bailey said, "People left Keystone because they didn't see any future there. There was no railroad and the roads were so bad they had no way of getting out except by team. So many left. Some went to Edmonton where there was work."

Douglas Breton was born in Simonstown, South Africa, in 1883. His father, a doctor in the British navy, moved to posts in various parts of the world, so Douglas was already well travelled when he arrived in Canada in 1904 at the age of twenty with his brother Laurence.

They homesteaded on adjacent quarter sections and began farming. They also worked for local sawmills and on the Grand Trunk Railway that was being built through the Yellowhead Pass.

In 1912 the Breton brothers built and operated the Telfordville store. When World War I broke out, Douglas Breton joined the Canadian Army and went to war. Having survived the war, he returned to Telfordville in 1920 with an English bride.

Since 1921, Douglas Breton worked to bring the railway through the Keystone farming area and then to link up with Edmonton while serving as president of the Telfordville Local of the Leduc District of the United Farmers of Alberta. He carried on his efforts after being elected to the Legislative Assembly for the Leduc constituency in 1926 as a member of the United Farmers of Alberta.

In December 1926, the Minister of Railways announced that the railway would be extended 22 miles from Hoadley to the new terminus to be named "Breton" in appreciation of the work done by Douglas C. Breton.

In 1927 I was six years old and the momentous event occurred. School was dismissed so that the children could witness the arrival of the first train to our area. The coming of the Lacombe and NorthWestern Railway created a burst of growth for Keystone, thanks to the tireless efforts of Douglas Breton. Only it wouldn't be Keystone anymore.

The land for the railway was purchased from my dad, Sam Hooks; and the tracks went right across our homestead on the west side. It was a good place to get water.

I have often heard that the NorthWestern line was better known as the Peanut line. The train made one trip each week from Lacombe to Breton, then returned the following day. It carried a mixed cargo. Its speed was a hair-raising 10 to 12 miles per hour. It was said that after the train passed Rimbey, the crew would stop the train and go hunting for prairie chickens and partridges in the woods while the passengers waited patiently in the "parlor" car. My sister-in-law Willie Hooks was one of those patient passengers once, and she was not amused.

With all its shortcomings, the railroad improved our living conditions. It put us on the map. But it wasn't free of tragedies. There were a number of train wrecks in our area, but the one I remember most took place when I was twelve years old. A terrible train wreck occurred when several cars derailed on a curve just outside Breton, killing two passengers and injuring many others. It became the main topic of conversation for weeks. Many years later, the old timers would bring it up and shake their heads sorrowfully. It was an incident burned into the brains of all those who witnessed that death and destruction.

Douglas Breton continued to serve as MLA for the constituency of Leduc until 1930, after which he farmed and served as secretary-treasurer for the MD of Pioneer #490. In 1934 he and his family moved to England where he died in February 1953.

With the coming of the railroad, businesses began to come to Breton: Woodcock's Cafe, Breton Hotel, and

Laurence Breton's grocery store. Rolla Ramsey moved his post office to Breton.

I can remember selling boxes of berries, usually blueberries, to the train crew. We often went to town to sell eggs to Mrs. Kelly's store and also took butter and vegetables to the Breton Grocery Store and Woodcock's Cafe.

It was at this time that Joe Hoath opened a blacksmith shop in Breton. Joe was a big, good-natured guy who always sported a black mustache and a smile. He came to Breton from the Iola district in Alberta with his wife Bertha and their seven children.[*] They pulled into Breton one day with all their household goods loaded on a hayrack drawn by a four-horse team of Clydesdales followed by a herd of thirty cows.

They had travelled sixty miles in five days and nights over swamp and muskeg on poorly marked trails to arrive at last at the land on which Joe homesteaded. On the trail it rained every day, turning the trail into a viscous gumbo and all but impassable. On one steep embankment, the load slipped out of control and slowly inched over the edge of a deep gulch. Joe Hoath and his boys jumped out ahead of the load and held it while Bertha Hoath braced it with a dead log.

Joe set up his blacksmith shop in Breton. He rented a house right behind our field across what is now the Sam Hooks Ravine. The younger children, Grenville, Merritt, and Kathleen, attended school at Funnell since there wasn't a school in Breton.

Joe's blacksmith shop was a much needed addition to the community. All farming was done with mules or horses over newly broken land that was full of rocks

---

[*] Phoebe, Kathleen, Bertie, Gervarenville, Lucille, and Merritt.

and stumps. It's no wonder the crude machinery often needed fixing.

For us kids, Joe's shop was a natural attraction. During the lazy days of summer or the bitter chill of winter, we would spend hours at the forge watching Joe manipulate the red hot iron rods that would be transformed before our eyes into parts needed to fix a plow, harrow, disc, wagon, or whatever. To us, Joe Hoath could fix and make anything. He did magic.

In later years we were all sad when Joe's blacksmith shop was torn down to make room for a curling rink. It was the end of an era with the demolition of that familiar landmark.

Sawmills were always important in the Keystone area; indeed, they preceded the founding of Keystone. The area abounded with some of the finest virgin timber in Alberta—Jack pine, spruce, birch, tamarack, and poplar. But the industry didn't really take off until the coming of the railroad. By then Keystone had become Breton, and the village entered its busiest phase.

As sawmills increased, the need for a nurse became evident. Jesse Fenton filled the bill. She sewed up wounded fingers, legs, and other anatomical parts that sawmill workers had a tendency to rip apart.

Jesse was born in Medicine Hat in 1902. After completing high school, she enrolled in nurse's training at the Medicine Hat General Hospital. A post-graduate course in obstetrics followed.

While on her first nursing job at the Lloydminister Hospital, Jesse was called to Wetaskiwin where her brother Bill lay gravely ill from peritonitis caused by a ruptured appendix. Doctors had given up hope for him.

There was no such thing as antibiotics at the time, and so only faith could save him.

Jesse was determined that he would not die.

"He shall not die! He's my brother," she repeated through muffled sobs. Determination drove the healthy young nurse; and throughout the night she worked unceasingly. He lived, Bill lived.

Jesse was dedicated to her profession. She accepted a position with the Alberta Government as a district nurse in the Buck Lake-Breton-Antross area. She covered her territory on horseback.

She married Charlie Evans and set up housekeeping in the Antross Lumber Camp. Jesse's training in obstetrics served the community well. The closest doctor was Dr. Hankins. He practiced out of Thorsby, 25 miles away—a fair distance in those days, especially when the weather was ugly.

The good doctor would come out when needed, but his territory covered a huge area, which included Calmar, Warburg and Breton. So he was on the go most of the time and was often paid in produce—chickens, ducks, turkeys, and a number of other commodities too numerous to mention.

As early as 1893 logs were taken from the Breton-Modeste area and floated down the Saskatchewan River to Walter's Sawmill in Edmonton.

In 1876, John Walter, an Orkney boat builder, settled in Edmonton across the river from Fort Edmonton, where he later established his sawmill. He had once been employed by the Hudson's Bay Company. Every spring logs would be floated down the river from the thick stands of timber west of Edmonton. Riding herd on the logs were great numbers of lumber men looking forward to a wild time in Edmonton.

But the wild times ended in the spring of 1915 when a flood hit Edmonton and swept away Walter's sawmill, logs, and lumber. His entire operation swiftly disappeared down the river. Lumber was picked up all the way to Lake Winnipeg, but none was ever returned to its rightful owners. This marked the end of John Walter's Lumber Company.

Dave Ricker's logging operation was one of the first around Keystone and one that sent its logs to Walter's Edmonton mill.

By 1910 his operation was in full swing working southwest along Poplar Creek during the winters. Logs were skidded out and hauled to the creek banks and left in skidways awaiting spring thaw. The logs would then be rolled into the water and floated to the Saskatchewan River. Some small dams were built on Poplar Creek when extra water was needed.

The Ricker Company ran an efficient operation and employed many of the homesteaders in the area. They also ran a store providing supplies and clothing that was brought in from Leduc and Wetaskiwin year round.

Building supplies and hay and grain for the work horses had to be freighted in as it was not possible to raise enough feed during the summer months. In the summer the company kept many of its men working on buildings and clearing land to raise feed for the livestock and produce for the workers.

The company built a log barn big enough to hold fifty horses. The roof over the large hay loft contained a built-in track to move loads of hay. A lean-to on the east end held grain for the horses Near the store was a large cookhouse and a number of bunkhouses. There was also a blacksmith shop, root cellar, and pens for a number of pigs used for meat for the camp. The pigs were fed scraps and waste from the tables. The buildings were all erected on the side of a spring that flowed winter and summer.

Then war broke out in 1914, and many of the young men left their homesteads to serve their country. Labour became scarce; but on top of that, the spring flood of 1915 that wiped out Walter's mill in Edmonton also dealt a death blow to Ricker's operation.

It washed out the dams and skidways on Poplar Creek. Logs were washed away and never recovered. This broke Ricker's logging company.

At the time Ricker had a large two-storey log house under construction. He already had on site fir flooring, good doors and windows, and sufficient bricks to build a fireplace and chimneys. He had planned to bring his family there to live. It was never finished and was later used by travellers on the road to Pigeon Lake.

After the flood, logging stagnated. The war had claimed much of the available labour, the mills in Edmonton were gone, and transportation was nonexistent, but with the coming of the railroad, things changed. The railroad made it economical to log and saw right on the location. Mills sprouted up all over the countryside. Among them were Anthony and Antross. Antross operated between 1926-1946.

In 1926 William Anthony Sr. bought a strip of timber located about 2 1/2 miles south of Breton on Poplar Creek. He began logging with horses.

He built a large modern steam-powered mill—extremely efficient according to the standards of the time. Sawdust and slabs, byproducts of the mill, were burned to make steam to drive the mill, while shavings were burned to power the planer.

The camp had several large bunkhouses, many smaller office buildings, a store, and a cookhouse.

D. R. Fraser and Company also operated a mill near Breton. In 1946, when I returned from the war, I went to work there.

The company was founded by Daniel R. Fraser and his brother Alex in Edmonton in 1881. Later his cousin John MacDonald joined the company and became a shareholder and director. John Fraser, 84, was placed in charge of logging operations.

D. R. Fraser and Company conducted its earliest operations close to Edmonton on tracts acquired from the Dominion Government, Department of Natural Resources, Edmonton. An office and yard were established on 97th Street, Edmonton, and became the head office for all operational planning and sales.

Logging occurred in winter. Horses were used for hauling logs and teamsters were required to groom their horses nightly.

When the Lacombe and Northwestern Railway came to Breton and was later extended to Thorsby and Leduc, the Fraser Company moved its headquarters to Breton, which experienced another mini boom period.

Schools were built and Ed Collins opened his bus service from Breton to Edmonton. Bill Spindler from Berrymore, Alberta, built and operated the Breton Hotel. Shortly after, the McGhies took over the hotel. Peter Nikiforuk opened a grocery store, and Tim Sexton bought the Breton Store. Don Jamieson opened the hardware store and the Pearson Brothers began a mill right across from Frasers'. A planer mill also soon went into service.

The railroad revived the logging and lumber industry. These in turn attracted businesses, and the village of Breton enjoyed a spurt of growth. In 1927 the Breton School, a small one-room school, was built on the south corner of our homestead.

My sisters Rose and Kathryn, my brother Richard, and I were among the first students. Mildred Ramsey was the only other black student. By this time blacks had become a minority in the place they founded and pioneered. Our first teacher was Dan McLeod.

He and his wife Alvena and seven children moved to Breton in 1928 from Iola. Dan McLeod taught in Breton for six years. Then he traded his house in Breton for a quarter section of land, began farming, and became Justice of the Peace.

One of our teachers smoked his pipe in class, a practice that would not be tolerated today.

My older sisters and brothers continued to attend school at Funnell. They walked miles through bushes and swamps, but Rose, Kathryn, Richard, Beatrice, Edward, and I just had to walk across our quarter. I took all of my schooling in Breton.

One of my teachers was Frances Hinds. She came to Breton from Calgary when her stepfather Walter Johnson and her mother Ida started a dairy farm on the outskirts of Breton adjacent to our farm. The dairy consisted of two milk cows. Walter sold his milk by going door to door and ladling out milk to his customers.

Frances, a city girl with no teaching experience, received her First Class Teaching Certificate when only nineteen and was accepted by the local school board to teach in the Breton School. On her first day of school, she faced 49 students of mixed race from grades one to nine. Not that this responsibility wasn't tough enough, she was also required to stoke and feed the wood-burning stove, an improvised oil drum that took large logs. The large room was poorly insulated and poorly sealed. It took a lot of wood to keep it warm.

An outdoor toilet served the calls of nature; and when the temperature dipped below the freezing point, it seemed that as soon as the room approached a tolerable temperature, someone had to make a nature call. This would let in a cold waft of air and create shivers throughout the room.

Once a parent complained to Miss Hind for not allowing her daughter to use the outhouse when she had to. Miss Hind explained that the toilet was only a two-seater and, at the time her daughter asked permission to go, both seats were already occupied.

Outdoor pumps supplied our drinking water. The water pails had to be filled several times a day. In our school, students all drank from the same dipper. On cold days, lunch pails (five-pound Swift lard pails) were lined up along a pipe barrier to thaw out. The barrier surrounded the stove to keep students from getting too close and being burned.

Discipline was no problem for Miss Hinds. She never used the strap, and we all tried to complete our assignments on time. She was a firm believer that "if you treat your students right, they will treat you right." We not only learned but we had fun too. Every Halloween and Christmas we would celebrate with parties and concerts.

Because she was a young and beautiful teacher, it's not strange that occasionally a student would become infatuated with her. And, of course that happened. One sixteen-year-old student was badly bitten by the love bug, and he fell into the habit of showering Miss Hinds with chocolates. Faced with the problem of discouraging this would-be suitor, she settled on a strategy that would cool his amorous inclinations toward her. Whenever she walked around the room examining students' work, she would stop behind him, examine his neck and quietly proclaim so that only he could hear, "Your neck is dirty!" This brought about an attitude shift on his part, and it wasn't long before he viewed her more like a mother than a lover.

Miss Hinds taught in Breton from 1930 to 1933 and then, while visiting a town in the Crowsnest Pass, she met a miner named Bert Bond. They fell in love and married. She joined him in the Crowsnest Pass and continued her teaching career there. Bert died in 1976. Francis still lives in Coleman, Alberta, retired after 30 years of teaching.

Chapter 8
The Great Depression

By the time the Depression came, the black population in the Breton area had diminished. Its numbers were further reduced as time progressed. The old pioneers passed away or retired to areas providing more modern facilities or better climates. Many of the young also moved away in search of better opportunities. But there still remained a sizable black population, making the area a distinctive community.

Charlie King was among those who stayed and served as a leader in the community until he died. He was a highly respected social activist, who became an important member and staunch supporter of the Cooperative Commonwealth Federation (CCF), founded in Calgary in 1932. This socialist political party later became the New Democratic Party (NDP), which he also supported. He later became personally acquainted with Tommy Douglas, socialist leader of the NDP. Various farmers' organizations gave the impetus to the new political party, especially the United Farmers of Alberta (UFA) of which Charlie was an active member. Charlie was chairman of the Breton Community Club for a number of years and Commissioner of Oaths.

By the 1940s, Charlie King had acquired a large amount of land and had become financially comfortable, but he never lost the common touch. He believed in a classless society, and he never placed himself above a fellow human being. He was, however, attracted to modern developments. As roads improved, he bought a 1929 Chevrolet. He was one of the first in the neighborhood to own a car.

Charlie was a man ahead of his time. His cool-headed wisdom earned him the respect of all who knew him, blacks and whites alike. At another time, in another place, Charlie could have stood beside men like Martin Luther King or Jesse Jackson.

Yes, we lived through the Depression, but it didn't make that much of an impression on any of us in the black community. Most of us were poor in good times as well as bad. It was hard to tell the difference. Everyone was in the same boat, so to speak; and we children just played with our friends and enjoyed ourselves.

One thing for sure, we didn't have to depend on soup kitchens or flop houses. We had our gardens and our livestock and a roof over our heads however humble it might be. And we had fun. There were always interesting things to do. Our community was a good place to live. There were a lot of activities such as skating on the creek, tobogganing, sleigh rides, hockey games, swimming, and ball games.

There were dances almost every week, and often we didn't pull into the yard in our cutters until the sun was peeking over the horizon. I used to love to listen to the hiss of sleigh runners gliding through the snow and the steady clop of our horses hooves, the smell of pine and spruce in the crisp air and the dazzling stars in the sky. The Depression didn't affect that.

We were well into the Depression when Dad decided to build another house. Lumber was cheap, so why not?

It was a grand house. It stood like a proud sentinel overlooking the ravine. It seemed huge to us, so used to living in our little cramped log cabin tucked into the side of the ravine. There were eight rooms to romp through. Mother was so happy because now she had a place where the family could all be together.

By this time most of the older children had left home and were working elsewhere, but all of them helped with expenses at home. During the Depression, I wasn't very old, but I can remember my parents struggling to make ends meet. But the house was like a big security blanket. It was a place where the family frequently came together and experienced many happy occasions. We thought it would always be there. We were wrong. It was destroyed by fire in 1974.

Rolla Ramsey operated the post office in Breton from a small, dark one-room shack with a single window on main street. But he didn't remain there long.

In 1936 he joined the number of blacks leaving the area and took his family to Rutland, British Columbia. We all missed them.

As children, my brothers, sister, and I used to play with the Ramsey children. One day, Viola Ramsey and I got into a terrible fight. She gave me the worst beating I ever had. I've never forgotten it. We would laugh about it on the rare occasions we saw each other.

When we were children, our house didn't have running water. We children had to make our way downhill through dense forest cover to the ravine for water and then carry it up the hill to the house. I've spilled many a bucket of water on that hill.

We kids used to play up and down the hill and in the bush around the house and barn. Sometimes we'd go hunting prairie chickens and bush hens, which were plentiful in those days. One seldom had to go without a meal.

One Sunday morning, when I was nine or ten, I decided to go hunting, although I should have been in Sunday School. Dad kept his guns on the wall behind the kitchen door. No one was around so I took a .22 and some bullets and slipped into the bush to a little knoll, which was part of the east-west highway. I had the gun cocked and ready for game. My finger nervously played on the trigger. I could see that rabbits had chewed a lot of little willow shoots and the butts were sticking up, so I knew they couldn't be too far away.

Well, I didn't see any rabbits, but my finger caught on one of those willow butts and the gun went off. The bullet went through the top of my shoe and lodged in the sole. I could feel warm blood oozing around my toes and I knew I was in a lot of trouble. I had to get home quick.

Mother was alone when I limped into the house. She saw me standing with the gun and blood pouring from my foot. "What on earth happened?" she shouted, "Dear God, help us."

I told her I didn't know where the bullet came from. Why I told her such a blatant lie I'll never know. Of course she didn't believe me, but she said nothing. She immediately whipped off my shoe and sock, cleaned the wound, applied some salve and bandaged it to stop the bleeding.

I was a lucky guy. It was only a flesh wound, and I had a wonderful nurse who knew just what to do as always.

In 1934 we lost our travelling nurse Jesse when her husband Charlie was transferred to Chisholm Mills, 110 miles north of Edmonton. Jesse kept as busy as ever there patching up torn bodies and delivering babies. She couldn't even travel in peace.

Once on a trip to Edmonton for a much-needed rest, a woman prematurely went into labour. Jesse was the only person on board qualified to handle the situation. She delivered the baby right there on the train.

After delivering so many babies for others, Jesse lost her only child at childbirth. She and Charlie later adopted a little girl named Colleen.

Jesse's entire life was devoted to helping others and she worked tirelessly toward that end. She passed away at 52, having worn herself out serving others.

Lillian Baynes, a registered nurse, filled the gap left by Jesse when she moved up north. The Baynes family, Walter and Lillian and their three children,[*] moved to Wenham Valley district in 1926. Lillian, like Jesse, was often called upon to render medical service to the sick and injured. She attended some terrible and bizarre accidents like the one where a boy had climbed a tree and fell onto a set of harrows. She was called to the death bed of several neighbors. Unfortunately, we lost her too in 1941 when she moved to Victoria, British Columbia, to live with her daughter Nellie.

Along with our public nurses, another institution had sprung up—one that struck absolute terror in my heart.

---

[*] Nellie, Joe, and Mary

It was the "Travelling Clinic" that the provincial government began sending out to small communities that did not have adequate medical facilities in the early '30s.

The clinics would move into town and set up their chamber of horrors. Then kids needing their tonsils or adenoids out were herded into the recreation hall. In Breton that was Nelson's Hall.

Among many other kids in the area, my sister Beatrice, my brothers, and I were all carefully selected as victims to go under the knife that day.

The setup was crude. A large curtain was drawn across the stage. Behind it was the surgical room. The big hall was filled with kids like wide-eyed calves waiting to be branded and castrated. When your turn came, a nurse came out and called your name and you followed her on rubber legs and disappeared behind the mystery curtain.

I could hear kids back there screaming and gurgling. My curiosity was more than I could contain. I bolstered my courage, sidled up to the curtain, and took a peek. I saw a big tub splattered with blood. Tonsils and adenoids were being chucked into it, and there was blood everywhere.

That's all I needed. I said to myself, "They're not getting me in there!" I made for the side door right by the stage. It was open. "Now is my chance," I whispered to myself as I slipped out unseen. I bolted to the bush like a rabbit, slid down the ravine, and hid under a brush pile.

When my turn came, they looked and called and called. But no one answered. They soon gave up on me and turned their attention to easier prey.

That evening about supper time, I came out of hiding and slinked home. I was scared. I knew I was in deep trouble, but where else could I go? Mother was on me like a tiger. I tried unsuccessfully to explain, but she told me of all the havoc and inconvenience I caused. I said I was sorry, but I was glad I still had my tonsils.

After supper my kid brother started to hemorrhage. The doctor was summoned from the hall. Mother was scared out of her wits with good cause. The doctor came, stopped the bleeding and cleaned him up.

He eventually recovered, but he was sick for quite awhile. I kept my tonsils until after the war when I finally had to have them removed.

The Travelling Clinic

In the early nineteen thirties or so,
This fact I am told,
Travelling clinics toured the country,
Removing tonsils was their goal.

Now the clinic visited Breton,
In the old Nelson hall,
So children with infected tonsils,
Their parents were given a call.

Now Mark and his brother Ed,
Were some of the fated crew,
Their Mother told them how much better
They would feel when the process was through

When they entered the hall that day,
Behind the curtain the children did shriek,
So mischievous little Mark Hooks
Thought he'd just take a peek.

So he quietly moved the curtain.
In a tub tonsils were floating about,
there Mark was certain—
From this place he had to get out.

Silently he slipped through the side door,
Down into the ravine he flew,
He dug deep into a brush pile,
"He was keeping his tonsils, he knew."

Well, when Mark's turn rolled around,
They called and looked all about.
But Mark huddled under a brush pile,
"They're not taking my tonsils out."

Now late at night when Mark went home,
The family told him he had been bad,
But Mark Hooks gently stroked his throat,
Cause his tonsils he still had.

After he came home from overseas,
With tonsillitis he had a bout,
It wasn't until nineteen forty-six,
Mark had his tonsils out.

The Depression didn't seem to slow down the lumber industry. Antross was operating full swing in the mid-30s when Ross and Beard Lumber Company built a large mill housing two planers. Every winter Anthony and Ross operated bush camps to supply logs and lumber for the mills near the railroad. Most workers stayed in the bush in bunkhouses, but on Saturday nights many caught rides into Breton to take in a dance or visit the "watering hole."

All this action gradually wound down when a series of bush fires swept through vast stands of timber in 1937 and 1938. The 1940s witnessed the decline of the lumber industry. Timber was running out and loggers had to go farther afield to find good stands. The distance became too great for the industry to stay viable in the Breton-Antross area. The companies started to close down in 1946 and dispose of their property. Many of the buildings were moved to Breton and the houses were sold. My wife and I bought one and moved it 2 1/2 miles north of Breton on my brother Ellis Hooks' farm in 1947. It became our honeymoon home.

At the time I was still working for Fraser's and experiencing its decline as an important industry in the area. Gwen was teaching school in Funnell and enjoying it immensely. The school's small, rural, and informal atmosphere lent an element of comfort and familiarity, a security of knowing intimately everyone around you and of a routine that could be counted upon. But with declining enrollment, all that changed and in 1954 the Board of Education closed Funnell School and sent its students to Breton.

Gwen would have been transferred to Breton too but for a recent incident that pitted Breton's black and white population against each other. It came about because of a play the Breton Drama Club staged in the school. The black community took offense because it was a parody that negatively stereotyped them. Performers with blackened faces employed an array of racial slurs to amuse the audience. That did not go down well with the blacks, and a disturbance erupted that ended in court. In summation the judge admonished the community to respect one another. All parties agreed; and although this first and only serious racial conflict in the area was put to rest, there remained a residue of racial tension for some years to come.

That residue influenced some of the trustees on the school board to vote against Gwen's being transferred to Breton. They did not want a black teacher in their school however dedicated she had always proved to be in school as well as in the community. Gwen took that decision very hard, and it planted a tinge of bitterness in her that wasn't there before. Her outlook greatly improved when Warburg School received her with open arms. She taught there for twenty-two years, the last ten of which she served as principal of Special Education. Her last year before retirement was served at Breton Elementary School.

Chapter 9
World War II

When I first joined the army in October of 1941, I had never traveled farther from home than Edmonton. What a devastating experience to be away from home, family and friends, but there were many young men in the same boat.

I was stationed at Camp Borden, Ontario, when I got the mumps and was quarantined for a couple of weeks. From Camp Borden I went to England and from there to Italy.

When my brothers Elmer and Richard and I were in World War II, Mom was very upset. Whenever she got a letter from any of us, she would rush over to my sister Virginia's home to have her read the letter, since she herself had never learned to read.

I became attached to a unit known as the First Hussars. It first won its reputation as a fighting force in South Africa near the turn of the century and maintained that reputation in two world wars.

In September 1939, the First Hussars was the first non permanent unit in Canada to be called into active service. Later light tanks replaced horses.

I served with a tank regiment for awhile. Our tanks weighed 55 tons. In spite of their massiveness and heavy armor, the Germans were able to knock out many of them. The damage was done when the shell broke into shrapnel. Then it really damaged the tank, often killing members of the crew.

I became ill and had to leave the regiment. Later I was reassigned to operating heavy equipment. I served in France, Germany, and Holland and saw a great deal of action in Germany.

On one occasion when I was pushing a bridge across a channel, a sniper's bullet scorched my beret. The Lord was with me that day. That bullet came much too close. It unnerved me for a while; then I shuddered, said a prayer, and went back to work.

Another time I had to dig a ditch about 50 feet by 25 feet to bury dead German soldiers. German prisoners of war were ordered to throw their dead comrades into the ditch. When the ditch was full, I covered it over and became sick to my stomach. It was common to see dead soldiers everywhere, but this task was just too much.

I was in Italy the day a Breton boy was killed. He was John Funnell, Richard's son. It was a sad day—a boy from home. I also met Ken Levers and Laurel Fenneman in Italy. It was sure nice to see someone from home.

I was in Germany when the war ended and was discharged on January 23, 1946. I received the 1939-45 Star, Italy Star, France and Germany Star, the Defense Medal, and the Canadian Volunteer Service Medal and clasp.

It was good to be home again in a country free from wars and devastation, and I am proud to be among the many who helped keep Canada free, but those war memories will always be with me.

But all was not well at home. There still existed those in Canada who preferred to judge others by the colour of their skin rather than on their qualities as fellow human beings.

After I'd come home from overseas, Gwen and I went to a well-known Edmonton lounge. We seated ourselves and waited to be served. A long period of time passed. We were obviously being ignored. Finally I called the bartender and asked him why we had not been waited on. He said the management was reluctant to serve black people. I asked to speak to the manager. When he came, I told him I had just returned from overseas where I had been fighting to keep Canada free. I was steaming. He apologized and offered us free drinks, but we declined. I was too mad to remain there, so we walked out.

I attended the First Hussars Reunion in the mid-80s in London, Ontario. A service was held at Victoria Park near the Sherman tank "Holy Roller" that was being displayed. It brought to mind the memories of my comrades and the intensity of our motivations for enlisting—to preserve the same freedom for others that we so cherished for ourselves.

Chapter 10
Breton Post War

After I returned from overseas, I worked for Fraser's Lumber Co. for $1.50 an hour for about three years. In 1947 I married Gwen Day who had come to Breton to teach school at Funnell. When Cyril Pyrch, the superintendent, interviewed her at her home in Edmonton, he told her that if she accepted the position at Funnell, she would marry someone in the district and he wouldn't have to look for a teacher for Funnell again. Gwen told him, "No way." She wasn't marrying a farmer, but she hadn't met me yet.

In 1948, we bought Colin Campbell's farm. It had been the homestead of Rolla Ramsey. Campbell was very ill and in hospital. I looked after the farm when his wife visited him. After he died, we bought the farm as it was. With the farm we got three horses, some cows, pigs, chickens, two dogs and some cats and the grain in the granary.

Campbell was very fond of animals, most of which were his trained pets. Scotty the horse was one of his favorites. Scotty could open gates if they weren't securely latched.

I hauled water from a nearby spring for the house in a barrel on a stone boat pulled by Scotty. We left the water in the yard, and if the gate was not securely latched, Scotty would open it, drink all the water he wanted and then upset the barrel.

Bobby was a little black dog who idolized Campbell and would have nothing to do with anyone else. He followed Campbell everywhere. They were each an extension of the other. While Campbell was in the hospital, Bobby never stopped searching for him. Day and night he whined and searched. The night Campbell died, Bobby howled continuously. When we awoke the next morning, the howling had stopped. Bobby was gone. We searched everywhere, but in vain. He just disappeared and was never seen again.

After the war the number of blacks in the Breton area dwindled to a small minority. But roots are a powerful attraction and occasionally families would drift back to the old homesteads—to what once was their Keystone community.

That was the case in the early '60s when Mary Bailey and granddaughters, Robin and Reo Bailey, and a friend, Lil Hayden, and her daughter, Arla, moved back to Breton from Calgary. The girls had attended Breton Elementary School. After living in Breton four or five years they moved back to Calgary. Mary Bailey passed away in Winnipeg just before her 100th birthday.

Keystone's children spread throughout Canada and some went to the United States. Most did well for themselves and became well educated and productive members of society. Some became administrators in the federal public service, professional entertainers, educators, business people, doctors, scientists, lawyers, and judges.

Violet P. King, the daughter of John and Stella King, was one of those who became very successful. John and

Stella were in Keystone about eight years before moving
to Calgary. John had come to Keystone in 1911 with
Charlie King Sr. and his wife Matilda.

While at university, Vi excelled in the five-year
course leading to the degrees of B.A. and L.L.B. At the
same time, she also taught classical music.

At both the 1951 and 1952 International Students'
Service Conferences (ISS) held in Hamilton, Ontario,
Violet represented the University of Alberta. The ISS
was an organization that promoted goodwill among
foreign universities.

In 1952 Vi served as vice president of the Students'
Union and was a member of the Gold Key Society, an
honorary association of students who had made
outstanding contributions to campus life.

In 1953 Violet earned the distinct honor of being the
only woman in her law class at the University of
Alberta. She was also the first black lawyer to graduate.
Former Premier of Alberta Peter Lougheed graduated
at the same time. Vi was the second woman in Calgary
to be admitted to the bar in June 1954. She practiced law
in Calgary before going to work in Ottawa with the
Citizenship Branch.

She then moved to Newark, New Jersey, and later to
Chicago, Illinois, where she accepted the position of
Director of Manpower Planning and Staff Development
for the YMCA and was appointed Executive Director of
the National Council of YMCA's Organization
Development Group. She was the first woman to be
named to a top management position in the United States
National YMCA. After achieving so much, Violet lost
her long battle with cancer and died in 1981.

Alberta's first black provincial judge, Lionel
Locksley Jones, had his roots in Keystone. He was the

son of Jesse Jones and Ruth nee Lewis. Jesse Jones, we will recall, was one of Keystone's first teachers.

There were those black pioneers who settled black communities other than Keystone whose offspring later came to Breton to carry on the tradition started by the first settlers. Willard Robinson stands out as an example.

Willard, son of Shawnee Robinson, moved to the Breton area with his father and the rest of the family in 1952. They were from Prosperity, about 12 kilometres from the black community of Amber Valley, Alberta, in the Athabasca country.

The Robinsons originally came to Alberta from Oklahoma in 1910 when Shawnee was only five years old. They homesteaded in the Amber Valley area, one of the most successful black communities in Canada. The black settlers were not only excellent farmers, but they organized one of the best baseball teams in all of Alberta. They were terrors on the diamond.

In an atmosphere of hard work and hard play, Shawnee grew up, married Cecelia Lanning, bought a farm, and started raising a family.

Their children numbered four when Cecelia found herself carrying another child. It would be her last. The baby survived, but Cecelia didn't. Shawnee awoke to the harsh reality that he was now a single parent, left to care for five children, one an infant. Willard saw his mother for the last time when he was seven years old. Years later, he too would experience life as a single parent.

About eight years later Shawnee bought a farm near Breton. Three of his children graduated from Breton High School before leaving Breton to live in various places in Canada's West.

All of the Robinsons were musically gifted, especially Willard and Dave, his older brother. Dave married Lois Hooks, my brother Ellis' daughter. She was musical too and together they formed a band called Ebony. But they also kept their day jobs. Lois taught in the village of Alder Flats and Dave had a job with an oil company. Later, my son Wayne played in their band. They played at gigs throughout Alberta and what a band it was! They were great to listen to; they were great to watch.

Dave and Lois were a stunning couple. Handsome and debonair Dave led the band and tall, slender, willowy Lois was as exotic as the ancient Egyptian Nephritite. Her movements were smooth and graceful, and her voice had a depth and tenor that reached down to one's very soul.

Two powerful personalities like these were bound to clash; and when they did, it led to divorce. Lois continued to teach, her low satin voice filling the classroom, but this tightly wound spring was winding down. She was in her early fifties when cancer took her life.

Willard is the last Robinson left in the Breton area. He still carries on the musical tradition of the Robinson clan. He played in many bands throughout Alberta and eventually formed his own called "Willard and the Roadrunners."

For more than thirty years, Willard has played gigs all over the area and beyond and at 60 he still does. He and his first wife had four boys before they divorced. Like his father Shawnee, he found himself a single father trying to raise his boys. After many difficult years struggling alone and juggling his duties as a father, musician, and farmer, he remarried. He and his wife, Marguerite now operate a farm outside Breton where they manage a herd of about a hundred head of Limosine cattle. The boys are all married and have moved away.

Vant Hayes is the last of his clan in the Breton area. He now owns and operates a section of land near the original homestead his father filed on early in the century. He is the last black returnee.

Married to Ethel Wilson in 1959 in Edmonton, he and his new wife moved to Ladysmith on Vancouver Island, B.C. Their oldest daughter, Peggy, was born there.

Three years later Vant moved his family to Breton and bought a bush quarter three miles west of Vant's parents' farm. A few years later they bought another three quarters, which completed the section. The land was covered with timber and bush, and Vant had to cut a trail to the site where they would build their home.

Like his pioneer parents and grandparents, they carried lumber in by hand about one-eighth of a mile from a dirt road. They built a small house and an "outhouse" both with a million-dollar view that consisted mostly of timber land dotted with distant farms. The lights of Drayton Valley could be seen 25 miles to the west. On clear days the magnificent Rockies could be seen along the horizon. They also built a small log barn for their three heifers, a dozen ewes, and a few chickens.

Late one summer, a large silver tip grizzly bear appeared with the intent of enjoying a meal of lamb. Vant ran for his gun, got off a shot but only wounded the intruder which staggered into the bush. With the help of his neighbor, Cecil Ellis and his trail hounds, they followed the bear's blood-splattered trail for about a mile. When they caught up with the grizzly, the dogs immediately turned tail and dashed off in Vant's and Cecil's direction. The grizzly charged the two men. Just in time, Vant got off a shot that saved their bacon. The bear crumpled to the ground dead. It was the first known grizzly to be shot in the area.

Even though the 1960s were certainly well into the modern era—a time when men were walking on the moon—the Breton area was still a very primitive place.

In order to support the farm, Vant had to take a job on an oil rig. One night in mid-December 1964 Vant left home at about 10 p.m. He was scheduled to work the midnight shift on a rig about sixty miles away. That night Alberta experienced a record-breaking blizzard.

The wind began to blow with ever increasing velocity and the temperature suddenly dropped. Snow swirled madly and the night became bitterly cold. Ethel piled more and more wood in the kitchen cook stove, but nothing seemed to ward off the encroaching cold. She moved four-year-old Peggy out of the bedroom and onto the couch near the stove and then piled warm bedding on top of the shivering child. Ethel kept the fire going at full blast all night.

When morning came, the storm seemed to have gained even more strength. The radio issued warnings to stay at home. A couple of people were reported frozen to death. The wind chill was -105F. Worried sick about Peggy, Ethel kept the child under covers with a hot water bottle.

During the day she had to venture out to feed and check the livestock and chop and haul armloads of wood for the house. At intervals she would sit before the stove with her feet in the oven to thaw out before chopping and hauling more wood.

The wind found every crack in the house and dispatched cold throughout. It was 20°F on the indoor thermometer with fire blazing. The snow stopped, but the wind continued to build drifts, and it cut like a razor.

Where was Vant? Caught in the blizzard? Freezing somewhere?

She realized the possibility of even lower temperatures when evening came. How could she make the house warmer? By closing up the opening between the living and sleeping area. That was the answer! She searched outside and found some lumber and plywood to do the job. Soon a warming effect could be felt. It was now 45F inside.

At supper time Vant appeared in the doorway and stomped the snow from his boots. What a relief! He was safe and home. With him was a welcome purchase—their first airtight heater.

In 1975 Vant and Ethel stocked their lake with rainbow trout. When they netted them out in the fall, they were pleasantly surprised at how quickly they had grown in less than six months. A six-inch fingerling became a tasty 16- to 18-inch two-pounder. Due to the interest of other farmers with ponds or dugouts wanting to stock trout, Vant and Ethel applied for and received a commercial fish farm license. That allowed them to raise and sell trout for eating and also to buy fingerlings for resale to customers for their ponds.

This is the way they explained their operation:

> Before spring breakup of each year, orders are received; then with a special 300-gallon stainless steel tank, airstones and oxygen, we travelled to a large hatchery in Saskatchewan. We made the trip four or five times, as 25 to 60 customers placed orders. Some customers are waiting when [we] return. It's a most hectic time as we work as

quickly as possible. The fish are counted and placed in the customer's 45-gallon drum of water. Others are placed in heavy plastic bags with water that is then filled with oxygen and quickly tied tightly.

We bring all sizes from three inches to fourteen inches. Rainbow trout are the most popular, but we also bring brook trout and Arctic Char. We were the first to bring in Arctic Char to Alberta. We had to obtain a special permit.

The fish we raised for ourselves are usually netted in November or December. We sell some for eating but also keep a fair share for ourselves—fried, baked or smoked they are delicious. It is our intention to build our own fish hatchery some day.

Vant worked on oil drilling rigs in Ellesmere Island, Canada's most northern island. Between 1980 and 1990, Vant worked as supervisor for Dayon Alaska, building very large drilling rigs. In 1980 a second daughter, Christie Leanna was born.

In 1989 Vant built a larger house from lumber cut on his own land. He hired a portable sawmill and planer. The planer was quite an invention—an old school bus which could easily be driven where needed. The men shoved the rough lumber in one end and the planed lumber came out the other.

Vant and his family love nature, and they try to keep the land as pristine as possible. Vant says:

We cleared some land but the majority is still covered with trees. We believe in the 'natural environment' as much as possible. We enjoy the land and the wild life. Over the past several years, we have seen more and more wild Canadian geese nesting in this area. Some raised their young in the yard by a pond and associate with our many tame geese. It's so nice to see and hear them in the spring when they return.

Vant also farms the "home place"—the home his parents homesteaded early in the century. Five members of the family still own the farm—Vant, Nellie, Adrian, Orville, and Luvern. Vant is the only farmer, though, still continuing the Keystone legacy; and he is the only descendant of the black pioneers who continues to live in the community.

In September 1995, the Agricultural Service Board and the M.D. of Brazeau 77 recognized farmers who were still farming land held in the family for at least fifty years. Vant received a certificate honouring that tradition, and a large plaque inscribed with all the names of those honored was presented. The plaque now hangs in the Municipal District Office.

A lot of history has been made since the first settlers came to Keystone with their families and loaded wagons. Life changed as it must but with pride our family carried on the traditions handed down by our parents.

Gwen and I lived on our farm until early 1994; but because of my failing health, we had to give up the home we had known all of our 47 years of married life and the home in which we raised our two boys.

It was a home filled with happiness where I watched my children bloom and grow. How many times had I watched them, lunch in hand, scramble down the long driveway on their way to school.

To say that I was broken-hearted would be an understatement. I asked Gwen to make up some "For Sale" signs. When she had done this, I walked down the long driveway toward the highway and posted them.

**Farm for Sale
by owners
696-2142**

I stepped back and glared at the signs as if they were my enemies, and then sadly returned to the house. Sitting at the kitchen table I repeated numbly over and over again, "This is the saddest day of my life."

I didn't notice Gwen slip out of the house and take down the signs I had just put up. It was a nice gesture but it only delayed the inevitable, and in a couple of days, I had to retrace my steps and put the signs back up.

It was soon sold.

We were devastated as we walked away from that loving home toward the vehicle that would take us to our new home in Leduc. Years of memories raced through my brain and my heart swelled as though it would burst. I fought back tears in vain. And I knew my end was near.

On July 1, 1994, the Breton and District Museum installed a plaque in honor of my father Sam Hooks, who had owned the homestead on which Breton was built. The ravine was named "Sam Hooks Ravine." I was the only one of his ten children able to attend the dedication. I was very sick at the time, having just got out of the hospital with a bleeding ulcer. I kept saying, "I've got to go. I've got to go." I did and I was proud to be able to cut the ribbon at the unveiling, although there were moments when I didn't think I'd make it through the event.

But the summer day was kind. The breeze seemed to breathe me in and out and I was made one with all myselves: the rebel boy, the soldier, the farmer, the loving husband and father. All had merged at last and my heart filled with gratitude for having been lucky enough to live in and to serve a land like Canada where so many like me were able to live in freedom, peace, and prosperity.

Most of the forests were gone; but at the edge of the ravine where we stood, we could gaze down on the thick growth of poplar and spruce that stood stiffly creaking and groaning as the ceremony ebbed on.

Random bits of memory invaded my mind: fields of golden grain waving in the wind, grass so green it hurt your eyes, the smell of a wood-burning stove, the crispy cold of a winter day, the brilliant stars in the northern sky—these were the truths that bathed my senses.

And I knew this was the place prepared for me, where at last this sacred earth would set my body free.

I thank God for such a loving family. Shortly after the ceremony, I was returned to the hospital. There was my family standing at my bedside. My loving wife, Gwen, never left my side. I have so much to be thankful for.

Mark passed away in his sleep on October 23, 1994. He was laid to rest in the Field of Honour. He was the first black person to be buried in the Breton Cemetery. One of the largest funerals in Breton, it was a full military funeral, attended by many Legion dignitaries and friends.

At last Mark's journey was over. He rests in the place he loved so much—Breton.

Your Love Will Remain in Our Heart
by
Gwen Hooks

Mark, we have lived a life of joy
But there were hardships along the way,
We worked out our problems together,
And hoped for a better day.

Mark, you were a loving husband
A father and grandfather too,
I'm so glad God granted me
A husband as dear as you.

We prayed for you when you were suffering,
But God knew what was best.
So He folded you in his Loving Arms,
Now you have eternal rest.

But we will live with our memories,
From these we will never part.
Dear Mark, your family loves you,
And that love will remain in our heart.

BIBLIOGRAPHY

Berton, Pierre. *The Promised Land: Settling of the West 1896-1914.* Toronto: McClelland and Stewart, 1984.

Billington, Ray Allen. *Westward Expansion: A History of the American Frontier.* Third Edition, New York: The Macmillan Company, 1967.

Breton and District Historical Society, The. *The Ladder of Time: A History of Breton and District.* Edmonton, 1980.

Canadian Encyclopedia.The. 2nd edition. Edmonton: Hurtig Publishers, 1988.

Carter, Velma and Akili, Wanda Leffler. *Window of Our Memories.* St. Albert, Alberta: B.C.R. Society of Alberta, 1981.

Forests to Grainfields. Berrymore Carnwood Historical Society. Calgary, 1977. p. 123.

Franklin, Jimmie Lewis. *The Blacks in Oklahoma.* Norman, Oklahoma: University of Oklahoma Press, 1980.

Hall, D.J. "Clifford Sifton: Immigration and Settlement Policy 1896-1905." *The Settlement of the West* edited by Palmer, Howard.

Palmer Howard. *Patterns of Prejudice: A History of Nativism in Alberta.* Toronto: McClelland and Stewart Ltd., 1982.

Palmer, Howard and Tamara Palmer (eds). *Peoples of Alberta: Portraits of Diversity.* Saskatoon, Saskatchewan: Western Producer Prairie Books, 1985.

Palmer, Howard with Tamara.Palmer. *Alberta A New History.* Edmonton, Alberta: Hurtig, 1990.

Index

Other Brightest Pebble books
you won't want to miss

Grand Delusions: Henry Hoet and Cobblestone Manor by James Musson is the true story of a great southern Alberta mansion and a reclusive artist from Belgium who spent fifteen years building it for the woman he loved. It is a story of love, obsession, creativity, tragedy, and insanity. It is a story of a monument to the human spirit that now stands as a Provincial Historic Site. This book was partly funded by the Alberta Historical Resources Foundation.

To the Town that Bears Your Name **by *Martin Nordegg*** is a story that takes place in 1912 when Martin Nordegg, the German-born entrepreneur and early Alberta pioneer who had discovered and developed coal deposits in Alberta's Rocky Mountains, takes his fourteen-year-old daughter, Marcelle, on a journey across Canada to Nordegg, the town that bears her name.

Martin Nordegg wrote this book for his daughter as a souvenir of their journey, that eventually ended on the Pacific Coast. He describes in loving detail the adventures they shared and creates a vivid picture of the country they crossed and a way of life that has already faded into history.

This book was partly funded by the Alberta Historical Resources Foundation.

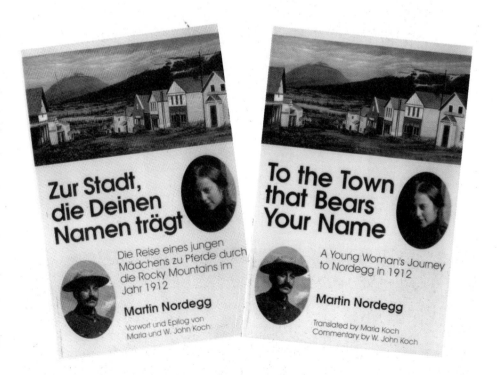

To Order

The Keystone Legacy:
Recollections of
a Black Settler

by

Gwen Hooks

Please send $12.95 plus $4.00 postage and handling to:

Brightest Pebble Publishing Co. Inc.
7604 - 149 Avenue
Edmonton, AB   T5C 2V7
Canada

Special prices apply for quantity purchases
of 10 or more copies.

For special prices please call (403) 457-7496
or fax (403) 475-0243

To Order

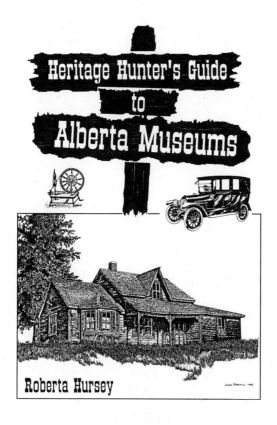

Please send $19.95 to:

Brightest Pebble Publishing Co. Inc.
7604 - 149 Avenue
Edmonton, Alberta, Canada
TSC 2V7

Phone (403) 457-7496   Fax (403) 475-0243
See order forms on the following pages

Please send the following book(s) to:

Name _____

Address _____

_____

Phone _____

No.	Description	Price	Total
	The Keystone Legacy	$12.95	
	Martin Nordegg: The Uncommon Immigrant	$19.95	
	Trailblazerr of Ukrainian Emigration to Canada	$16.95	
	Grand Delusions	$14.95	
	To the Town that Bears Your Name	$12.95	
	English Edition		
	German Edition		
	Heritage Hunter's Guide to Alberta Museums	$19.95	

Send cheque or money order to:
Brightest Pebble Publishing Co
7604 - 149 Avenue
Edmonton, AB TSC 2V7.
Phone (403) 457-7496 Fax (403) 475-0243

Please add $2.50 to your order for postage and handling.

Please send the following book(s) to:

Name _____

Address _____

_____

Phone _____

No.	Description	Price	Total
	The Keystone Legacy	$12.95	
	Martin Nordegg: The Uncommon Immigrant	$19.95	
	Trailblazerr of Ukrainian Emigration to Canada	$16.95	
	Grand Delusions	$14.95	
	To the Town that Bears Your Name	$12.95	
	English Edition		
	German Edition		
	Heritage Hunter's Guide to Alberta Museums	$19.95	

Send cheque or money order to:
Brightest Pebble Publishing Co
7604 - 149 Avenue
Edmonton, AB TSC 2V7.
Phone (403) 457-7496 Fax (403) 475-0243

Please add $2.50 to your order for postage and handling.